C000001458

What I Propose: John Ira Thomas
What Changing The Bible Gains Us

It is probably inevitable that when the JIT writes about the Bible, it will upset some people. But, after years of being pursued and harassed by people obsessed with a drawing based on two lines of that book, he has some conclusions to share. And they will surprise you. Does it make sense that we have not gleaned anything new about the Bible's text for so long, yet the text has remained unchanged for centuries? "What I Propose" is a call to make the Bible better for everyone.

147

Also in the 2021 Annual...

Did you know? 3 fun facts about this issue.

1. This issue exists because someone mailed John a chair.
2. Keller Sandoval is already awaiting sentencing for her idea.
3. Michael Loum believes that God like to finger Oklahoma.

TIRE

is now over one hundred years old, and has only ever been about two things—tires and the New Age. It's flipped between those things a couple of times now, but anything a century old is going to be a little unpredictable. After this, *TIRE* will go back to being about tires. After that, it'll probably disappear. As the person responsible for most of the flipping, I want to say that it's been a privilege to play around with something that has had such a long life. If I want to mess with anything this old again, I'll have to go put stupid hats on redwoods. Once again, I am the entire editorial staff for the issue. I didn't do it in a month, like last time, because I'm twenty years older and you don't get faster at things like that. I'm not including subscription information, because the Venn diagram of people who will want to read this issue and the next looks like headlights. If you want more of this, you'll have to bother me personally. Ruth doesn't seem to mind if I make more. But I can't say for sure, mostly because I've been explicitly told that speculating on Ruth's motives will net me a visit from lawyers. And I respect lawyers too much to force them to explain to me the very obvious facts of this world. So here's more *TIRE*. Let's leave it at that.—*JIT*

Normally, this is where the contact information for *TIRE*, such as email, website, physical address, etc. would go. But as a favor to the extremely nice assistant editor of the current incarnation of *TIRE*, I'm not going to sic you people on her. She doesn't care in the slightest about your manuscript, your product, or your path to Nirvana. If it isn't about tires (and they do a ctrl+F on everything they receive to make sure that word is used), it goes in the garbage. I am legally required to state that the editor-in-chief of *TIRE* is still Ruth Corley Watt, so I just did.

This part is where the info for advertising inquiries go, and I'm sparing the current *TIRE* regime that indignity as well. They're a corporate magazine. They overcharge for ads and get their price, because the tire industry is a small place and nobody wants to look cheap. I had to run a regular tire ad in this issue and I wish I got the cash for that. I had to settle for having fun near it. So, the headline here is: don't bother *TIRE* about this issue.

TIRE ANNUAL 2021 was written, designed, painted, and drawn by John Ira Thomas, with illos, designs, and design wisdom from Carter Allen, Will Grant, Ben Kirbach, Jeremy Smith, and Vivian Anne Wall. Special thanks to Ben Kirbach and Lisa Martincik for proofs and sage advice. Photos for the *New JITV Commentary* are by John Ira Thomas, Carter Allen, and Terry Farr (plucked from their Facebook feeds with permission). Pet Coven pics by Jeremy Smith, Carter Allen, Jerri Shaw, and Lance Cheung (for the USDA—public domain). Meat pic by Austin Allen Hamblin. Columnist pics are Danielle Crawford, Austin Allen Hamblin, Kayla Hamblin, Bethany Jackson, Ben Kirbach, Lisa Martincik, Joe Pray, and JIT.

THIS ISSUE'S CONTRIBUTORS

RAINER INMER is an Elk, a Moose, an Eagle, a Knight of Pythias, a Knight Templar and an Odd Fellow (I.O.O.F.). He holds an up-to-date real estate license and wants to talk to you about the Modified but Ancient Order of the Golden Lawn.

JILLANE SIF HENFORSAKER knows enough about physics to change the world. Her latest book, *PARTICLE INTIMIDATION AND THE END OF TINY DAYS* is very clearly mapped out in her head. She can also tell you which star is her father.

KURMASANA STEVENS is the heir to a yogic empire, which sounds like there's a weird sprawling temple involved. But there isn't. It's two condos and a lot of work.

DILLANE CZECKI has a degree in "scientific," a course of study that involves "applying science to things." After abandoning work on deprecating the liver, Dillane has focused on applying science to other organs.

ELIJAH LAND FREEMAN is a homeschooled lawyer who graduated at the top of his class. He spends his time generating an enviable torrent of threatening letters. He is very handsome and I'm sure he smells nice.

ADEL HOYT-KELL is the first licensed macropsychologist, as well as the head of the first macropsychologist licensing body. His favorite color is yellow, for scientific reasons.

MARATHON JOSHI is a bit of a jumble. He studied Classics and wants to use that knowledge to create not so much a system of morality as a morality test that anyone can use. It remains to be seen if money can be made on actual morality.

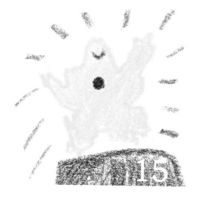

MEGACONTEMPLATIONS
The First Story After the Picture

Written and drawn at the Orlando Megacon, this work represents the first Jitting since the original drawing. It is reprinted here in its entirety from the out-of-print Candle Light Press edition.

JOHN IRA THOMAS

JITTING
After "The Fall and After"

Written, drawn, and painted for this issue, this work expands on "Megacontemplations 2: The Fall and After" from *TIRE June 2000* by expanding into a new artistic medium.

JOHN IRA THOMAS

THE NEW JITV BIBLE COMMENTARY
Coming to a Truckstop Near You

It's a new kind of Jesus tract, one specially tuned to the Bible issues of John Ira Thomas. He's always wanted to make one of these things, and he's finally found a good reason to put more Bible knowledge into the world.

JOHN IRA THOMAS

ERIT, Summer 2021
A Zine Devouring Itself

Whitney Allen Turner's worst enemy wrests partial editorial control and wreaks havoc in the only zine dedicated to the destruction of the Anti-JIT.

JOHN IRA THOMAS & WHITNEY ALLEN TURNER

130

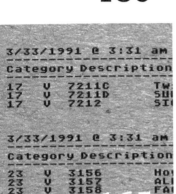

165

174

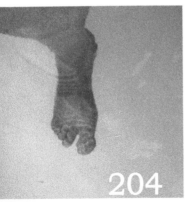

204

COLUMNS

DEPARTMENTS

I. Oujai

I know what you're thinking. Did another Corley die? Why am I doing another issue of *TIRE*? Is this another opaque legal move by people I will never see or meet to gain benefits I will never experience? Is this an Abrahamic test? Will someone intervene right before I submit this thing and tell me they just wanted to see if I would?

I would never have done this again without the chair. A Corley Logistics panel truck dropped it off at my house one sunny day during the 2020 quarantine and I knew the whole damn thing had started all over again. My first thought was that Ruth Corley Watt had died. I can't say I've seen much proof of Ruth's continued existence, but I am assured that from a "don't rile the stockholders" point of view that such speculation is irresponsible and actionable.[1] But, *TIRE* was a ritual associated with death in my mind at the time.

The chair was from the little house on Corley Street in Akron, the offices of *TIRE* magazine. It's an old steel and leather industrial model that sits in my home office as I write this. It's a great chair.

Strapped on the seat of the chair was a red plastic briefcase full of square data cartridges and an internal drive to read them. There was no letter, no note, no indication why I'd received this, other than the waybill inside the case. The "decription" (a clue?) of the contents of the shipment were itemized as "CHAIR" and "CONTENT."

THE JIT

is here to tell you why you're here.

#171 on card

Once I'd rigged an IDE to USB connection and worked out the voltage for the drive, I started looking through the cartridges. These were heavy-duty storage. Each one had a single enormous PDF file. It was the contents of the little house on Corley Street—every scrap of paper, every letter sent in, every page of every book sent in for review. Some poor bastard had been tasked with scanning all of it. I've seen her hands, caught in an ill-timed flip on the 312th page of another goddamn explanation of the Great Pyramid. I wonder about her often.

It couldn't be Ruth, I thought. It couldn't be. But all I have is the impression that rich people have...a lot to do? Shit, I thought. It could be Ruth.

I eventually saw the order to do all the scanning. The mystery scanner had inadvertently scanned that too. It was some noise about corporate data retention, but it made no sense. Why keep the entire contents of a dead magazine, right down to the owner's manual for the coffee pot?

TIRE isn't exactly dead. It reverted to being the tire and rubber industry journal it had been before it became the thing that wrecked my life. But there's a whole magazine about that already. The current *TIRE* is only related to the old *TIRE* by

Studies of a mystery box. I took these after I hacked off the pallet and brought the chair into my office. I would have done an unboxing video, but I was frankly too weirded out.

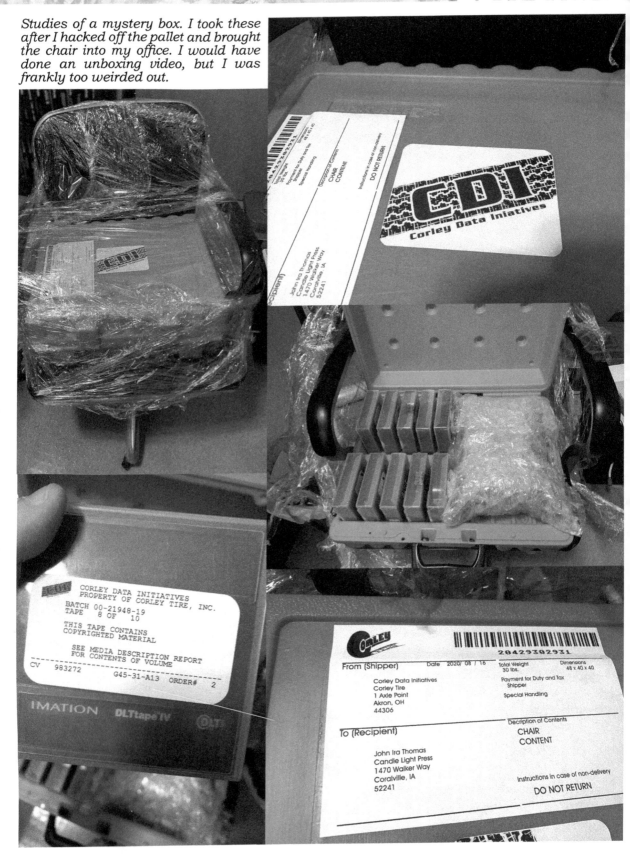

CORLEY DATA INITIATIVES
PROPERTY OF CORLEY TIRE, INC.

BATCH 00-21948-19
TAPE   8 OF 10

THIS TAPE CONTAINS
COPYRIGHTED MATERIAL

SEE MEDIA DESCRIPTION REPORT
FOR CONTENTS OF VOLUME

CV   983272   G45-31-A13   ORDER#   2

IMATION   DLTtape IV

From (Shipper)   Date 2020/ 08 / 16   Total Weight   Dimensions
                                                30 lbs.   48 x 40 x 40

Corley Data Initiatives   Payment for Duty and Tax
Corley Tire   Shipper
1 Axle Point   Special Handling
Akron, OH
44306

                                                Decription of Contents
To (Recipient)   CHAIR
                                                CONTENT
John Ira Thomas
Candle Light Press
1470 Walker Way   Instructions in case of non-delivery
Coralville, IA
52241   DO NOT RETURN

28429302931

name. They share no DNA. They don't even make it in Akron anymore. The little house on Corley Street isn't there anymore. (I occasionally look in from on high via Google Earth on days I can hardly believe I was ever there.) All that was left of the *TIRE* offices as I knew it was a chair and some ludicrously large PDFs.

But why send this stuff to me? If it was really about corporate data retention, the case should be in a salt mine and the chair in a hipster second-hand store. I tried calling the number on the waybill. All they would do is confirm that I received the pallet. "Right," I said. "I know that. I received it." They repeated that they could confirm that. So at least we could agree on that point.

Corley Logistics was listed as the sender, but they couldn't or wouldn't say who made the decision to send it. This had gotten ridiculous. It had to have been Ruth. But why?

I had no love for *TIRE*. I had even engaged in a bit of vandalism at the office back in 2000, torching the *TIRE* back issues in a barrel in the backyard during a dark night of the soul. I called it a cleansing ritual, but the firemen who showed up chose other words.

I hit the Corley Tire Company phone tree and got all the way up to Ruth's assistant, a very nice person who was an impermeable wall when it came to getting at Ruth. She conceded that her name was Alden (along with her pronouns), but I could get little else from her, until I mentioned the chair.

"You're the JIT, then," she said. "We should begin again."

Long pause. My turn. I asked *why send me a chair?*

"WHY send you a chair? Or why send you a CHAIR?"

I should have hung up and pushed the damn chair and case into the Iowa River. But I smelled an opponent with a decision tree and a desire to follow orders exactly. Ruth had me in her clutches again.

Is this payment for services rendered in 2000?

"There were no outstanding payments owed to you."

Are you going to send me a bill for this stuff?

"You have no outstanding balances."

Is this a gift?

"Gifts are not delivered by Corley Logistics."

Does Ruth want another issue of TIRE?

"That would be a decision for *TIRE* Editorial to make."

That's not what I asked.

"I can't speak to what Ms. Corley Watt wants unless she states her preference."

Alden was as trapped as I was. She was too exacting to have gone rogue and sent this stuff herself. She was confined to describing the world as it appears, and that's no good for working out the motives of the unseen and the unknowable.

Am I going to hear from any lawyers about the chair and the case?

"That depends on what you do with them."

Is Ruth dead?

"No, and you may hear from the lawyers about that." I did.[2]

The lawyers were not open to my pesty questions, even when I offered to pay for their time to answer. They don't divide their hours into 60ths and they have better things to do.

On my second call with Alden, I asked what she would do if she had received this stuff.

"I'm not you. But you don't seem the sort of person who needs a roadmap."

A compliment?

"I don't think it is, no." Alden is a really good assistant.

Okay, a new *TIRE*. It's the only possible thing Ruth could want from me.

I had one other theory. I did wonder if it was an offering for me, to give me the opportunity to destroy what was left of *TIRE*. But these were representations of *TIRE*, copies. It was a sign that whatever else was left of *TIRE* was being kept far away from me. But the chair was the editor's chair, the one her father sat in.

I don't have to grow her father's mustache and wear a dashiki, do I?

"Ms. Corley Watt is not seeking cosplay." Alden occasionally became politely impatient with me, but she never ever ended the call. And I called a lot.

You couldn't have paid me to do another issue of *TIRE*. The last time damn near killed me. But it was the only thing Ruth could possibly want from me. Her first move was to send me a chair. My first move was to wander around like a dumbass and deny the clear sign I'd been sent.

II. Legitima

I contacted the current assistant editor of *TIRE*—a very easy person to reach, as she's probably the only person on salary there. The magazine business is brutal. Ruth is still editor-in-chief, for reasons too long to get into here.[3] But the assistant editor of *TIRE* runs the daily business of the magazine, and she is a gentle soul who has no idea why I would want direct feedback from Ruth. If I had her job, she'd be right. Attention from bosses, bypassing many layers of supervision, is guaranteed to be bad news. She's never been told what Ruth wants either, but she knows she has a tire magazine to run.

The current *TIRE* is even less like the original *TIRE* than the original was to the New Age version. Gone are the letter columns, a back alley where people who knew way too much about tread and splay fought like animals. There is no research presented, just bullet point synopses that read like ads. The last issue was 36 pages. I've stapled fatter zines in my sleep. It's a hollow shell. The current assistant editor isn't to blame. She's supposed to make a magazine and this is what's available. There's a web version, but it's just a PDF of the print one. It's all very sad.

So *TIRE* is now something mailed to corporate offices and placed in view so other corporate types don't think you're some ignoramus who doesn't subscribe to *TIRE*. In ten years, even that conceit will be gone. And if the information isn't sticky, meme-ready, or about how everything you know is wrong, it will never reach the people who need to know it. I'm not here to defend corporate publishing. I'm here to defend a record of knowledge. We like to think posting something online is permanent, but where's everything posted on the Prodigy BBS now? We like to think preserving online history is a settled problem, but it's not.

So, I decided there would be another physical issue of *TIRE*. Not a mere magazine, but an annual. *TIRE* had stopped doing annuals when Arthur Peyton Corley died. They were a lot of extra work, a thirteenth issue wedged into a publication year. Even comics don't do them anymore. But I'd be damned if I was going to repeat myself. If there was to be another issue of *TIRE*, it would be an annual.

And it would be a joint publication by Corley Tire Company and Candle Light Press. Ruth's goal here (whatever it is) isn't sales, and I wanted to do a few things that might have been a hard sell to Ruth and her lawyers. And, as it turns out, Candle Light Press had something it wanted to do too (see page 104). Everybody wins!

If you bought this expecting to read about tires, you can console yourself by knowing that you are at least a proper *TIRE* completist. There's nothing in here about the tire industry. Oh, except one thing. One advertiser in the current *TIRE* has a contract that their ad must appear in every issue in 2021, so I had to run that unmolested. And if you know me at all, you know I do whatever three lawyers tell me to do.

So, in the current *TIRE* I found inspiration. The old staff of the previous *TIRE* wouldn't even talk to me. I thought I might glean something from how Arthur Peyton Corley ran things. But they seem to be living in the JIT tribulation. The seals are open and the Anti-JIT freely roams the earth. After all, *TIRE* as they knew and loved it went up in flames and I was there to piss on the ashes.

And in the ashes I found a sketch by some despairing staffer who satirically meshed the two *TIRE*s by depicting the Earth as the axle of a steel-belted radial rolling through the universe. I had Will Grant do it up nice and made it the cover of this issue. You hear that, *TIRE*? Even death is no escape from me. Also, you've got no room for satire when you take all this junk seriously.

III. Mishpat

When Candle Light Press reprinted the June 2000 issue of *TIRE*, I went out and sold the thing. I found quickly that either the customer was on board immediately or it was no dice. Reviewers across the board declined to review it. When asked, they said they liked it (or said nothing). Even the damn awards people couldn't decide if it was Humor or Religion. But they ignored it in both categories, favoring a joke book and a romance novel where someone bangs an angel. So why do another *TIRE*? I have an audience of one. She mailed me a chair and the platonic form of the *TIRE* offices and brothers and sisters, that's a sign.

But this is where belief gets me into trouble. When your peers find out you generated an entire issue of a New Age magazine in a tormented month because you were thrown out of Sunday school as a kid, a gap forms between you and the world. It's like finding your best friend gnawing a hole in the belly of a dead deer when all you wanted was to borrow the Wi-Fi password.

Religion remains the wildwood that it was invented to navigate. Religion is the old house, the shed that the bees took over, the guy sitting on the sidewalk asking for spare change. For most people, religion lives in the edge of vision. For most people, it takes something serious and unavoidable to address it at all. Even ancient or, to be honest, recent atrocities are not enough. It's hard to get people to speak in a real way about what they think might be out there.

This, too, may slide by like a shadow. That doesn't mean it's not meant to be. I damn well mean it.

And don't think I didn't see the spate of throwbacky ads shoot through the few remaining print New Age mags over the last couple years. I advertised *TIRE June 2000* in those same magazines and was amazed at how cowed they seemed. There was very little pizzazz. So I livened things up with my ads and others followed suit for a bit.

New Age mags now are acutely aware of how they used to sound. There is not one article now that doesn't include an acknowledgment along the lines of "I know this sounds crazy...". Does that sound like a true believer to you? If you start with an apology, you're not selling. There's no urge to widen the circle.

In the absence of a world of people trying to share their knowledge or simply trying to get your dollars, the focus of these magazines has turned inward. A magazine was once the best way to take a lot of specialized information and dispatch it to interested readers. Today, that's the Internet. So the magazines went from being run by someone who wants to serve as a focusing lens to the last of the sellers turning magazines into catalogs of their own product—paper websites. They are no longer snapshots of a period of time. They are snapshots of what's currently in stock.

The book you hold in your hands now[4] needs to exist. We all have our reasons. And we don't always need to know why.

IV. Sin

I would end on a semi-profound note, but I have to tell you about the card. You'll really enjoy this (unless you're an advertiser).

My first thought on soliciting ads was to hit up the old *TIRE* mailing list. But those folks are all out of the game. Those cons went back to television. TV preachers (can you *believe* TV preachers are a thing again?) now sell you colloidal silver and bits of the body of Christ in gel capsules and promise to hold off the cancer a little longer. They're not looking to get into print ads.

What I realized while scamming for ads is that a lot of people do them for free anyway. If you flip through one of the current mindfulness digests, it becomes clear that the advertisers are the columnists. This enables the magazine to appear to have a large rotating staff, while the advertisers get more ad space without

appearing to be an ad. And not appearing to be an ad is the whole ballgame these days.

The advertisers do one-page "columns" about their scam, then put the contact info at the bottom of the page as if it was their vitae. The other thing I noticed was that they always submitted three columns, because they wanted to show that they could write about a range of topics besides their main hustle. Dangling the possibility of a regular column to pitch their wares was enough to get a huge pile of submissions.

Even though they knew the columns were just scams to conceal ads, loads of these people tried to get a job they knew to be imaginary. Because there's nobody easier to scam than a scammer. They stay pretty busy fooling themselves. So I put out a call for columns, and approved one of the tryout columns instead of their withheld "official submission".[5]

Instead of having to go to all the effort of redacting key elements of hundreds of ads to keep anyone from giving these people any money, I decided to be a nice guy this time and make it convenient for everyone. Each columnist and ad has a three-digit number corresponding to a number on the enclosed ad response card. If anything in here interests you, just circle the number on the card and drop it in a mailbox. The postage is paid, and the info will be mailed to you. But you can only use the card. Requests made not using the card will be ignored.

Oh, and there are no classified ads. Those have been gone for a while. You can't sell the damn things anymore. Scamming for extra stamps just doesn't make sense in the era of email.

So, don't forget to fill out your ad response card. A lot of people worked really hard on their pitch for their fake bullshit, and it would be a real shame if even one of those cards never came back. Even bullshitters have feelings.

Endnotes

1   Which is exactly how the letter from the lawyers put it.

2   I am not allowed to speculate on this point without adding that such activity is reckless and only employed as a humorous trope with no basis in fact.

3   The editor-in-chief of *TIRE* must also be the CEO of Corley Tire Company. See the introduction to *TIRE June 2000* for the whole story.

4   Unless you're reading a pirated pdf from booksplooge, et. al., in which case you are not absorbing the special watermarks prepared for the paper edition that are designed to keep your mind and soul open for higher knowledge. Reading a bootleg PDF of this is like watching your soul masturbate to a picture of a cat. Some of us are trying to advance in the universe, so if you're not holding a real book right now, cheapskate, just keep wanking at Mr. Whiskers. A spent, distracted soul will be a big help in netting you yet another round on the prime material plane.

5   Because, and I cannot stress this enough, fuck those people.

Start a lodge! Crowley did it. Why not you? Plenty of fraternal lodges are a generation out from extinction. Odd Fellows, Elks, Moose, Knights of Pythias, Daughters of Job—the field is wide open and so are the real estate opportunities. Get in on the ground floor of the next wave of lodges!

Let's face it. Fraternal orders are passé. Somehow, wearing a fez isn't as fun as it used to be. And the young just aren't joiners. They want to connect online, through social media, or not at all. And lodges of all stripes are suffering.

In this suffering there is opportunity. The last member standing in a lodge can rebrand an entire order in their image! Not feeling it as an Odd Fellow? Rewrite the Book of Forms! Not wild about the Knights of Pythias logo? Slap some bezants on there! Who's going to stop you?

Most of these societies are late American creations, so there's no governing body that's going to stop you. All you have to do is get the membership fees coming in. They'll let you do anything! *Crowley* did it. Why can't you?

The Benevolent Protective Order of Elks was founded in the mid-19th century. Same with the Shriners. These are hardly ancient sects. The Order of Demolay's ritual was written in the forties by a newspaperman in Kansas City. *You* can start a lodge!

Once you find a suitable lodge, you'll need to join. Many operate on the blackball system and can be tricky to approach through normal channels. I became an Odd Fellow by reading the Book of Forms and knowing more about their rituals than the members did. Most of them couldn't tell an Outside Guardian from an Indoor Sentinel. Many of the lodges with more complex rituals don't bother at all anymore! I just started the rituals, and the rest of the members fell in by muscle memory. When I told them my membership card had been lost, they minted one on the spot. Initiation or no, if you pay them membership fees, you're a member.

I currently belong to eleven different lodges in three cities. I've rebranded a Moose lodge into a delightful Golden Dawn offshoot with fewer sexual demands and more staring at the sky waiting for the Fourth Book of the Law to manifest. We have a fine time waiting for the next age of flying saucers!

Some lodges are trickier than others to infiltrate. But I have assembled a handbook for methods to quickly and efficiently join everything from the Daughters of Job to the really tricky ones like the Scottish Rite. Just circle 193 on the contact card for more details! What are you waiting for? Get your confusing and murky notions of the universe to start working for you!

Rainer INMER thinks you're ready to start a lodge.

#193 on card

I've been to Sunday school once, and was invited not to return. Thirty-plus years ago, I drew the image on the first page of this book and that sealed my fate among the Baptists. Normally, the Baptist faith is about making an adult choice to be baptized and thereby join the church. Sometimes, they make the choice for you.

You've probably already flipped the page to find out if it's obscene, confrontational, or blasphemous. All I remember is that I was to draw what we learned that day. "The God of the King is going into the lion's body." For years, religious friends have made a game of trying to see what Bible verse I was interpreting. Most assume Daniel in the lion's den, but they're never happy with it.

Try **2 Kings 17:26**—"It was reported to the king of Assyria: 'The people you deported and resettled in the towns of Samaria do not know what the god of that country requires. He has sent lions among them, which are killing them off, because the people do not know what he requires'" [NIV edition]. I can see me thinking about the Samarians using a lion to determine the strange god's will.

My mother, who taught Sunday school years before, shrugs off this speculation. She and my father always told people that I was dropped off by a spaceship, and that my alien's-view of the world was par for the course. It would only have surprised her if I'd done something normal.

THE JIT

might have tampered with this reprint a bit.

#167 on card

Many years later, I drew the second image in this book for Jeremy Smith, my great friend. But the rest of the images and story in this book came from sitting at my Artist Alley table at the wonderful 2012 Megacon. I simply wondered what the rest of the story was.

I was walking from the motel to the convention hall on the second day of the convention, when my path took me by a Walgreen's. I immediately turned from my path, went inside, and strode up to the school supplies section. The crayons were in my hand before I had any sense of why. When I started looking for rough yellow paper to draw on, I knew what the day held for me. I was to continue the story in the Samaria of my imagination.

The next year I was back, selling this book. I explained all this to a woman who walked up and she froze up on me. "You know the mysteries?" she asked. I said I knew about the Eleusinian Mysteries. Silence. To break the ice again, I stuck out my hand and said "My name's John." She took my hand, said "I think I have to get away from you" and backed away, still clutching my hand. I had to pry her hand off mine to keep her from pulling me across the table.

And that's what it's like being the JIT. Jealous?

MEGACONTEMPLATIONS

a fragmenta fable

John Ira Thomas

The God of the King
is going into the lions
body.

The Lion's Redemption, and the God swims to Light Fallen

The lion of the God spreads his MANE over the SHAPELESS grey things, but his light cannot reach them.

While the mane would not touch the world, each glowing hair TANTALIZED the grey kings, as the LION HIMSELF seemed to hang from each of his own hairs, beckoning.

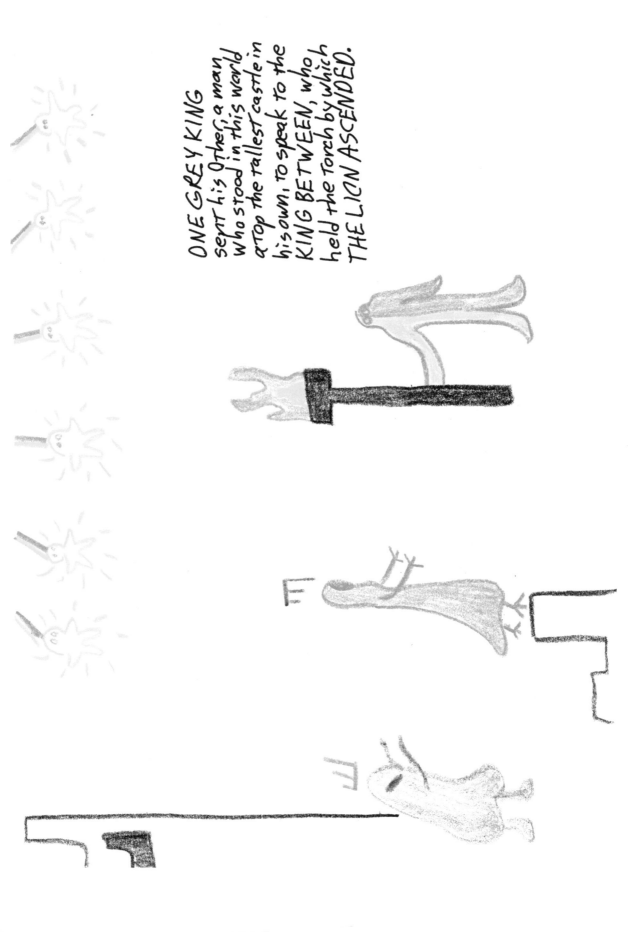

ONE GREY KING sent his Other, a man who stood in this world atop the tallest castle in his own, to speak to the KING BETWEEN, who held the torch by which THE LION ASCENDED.

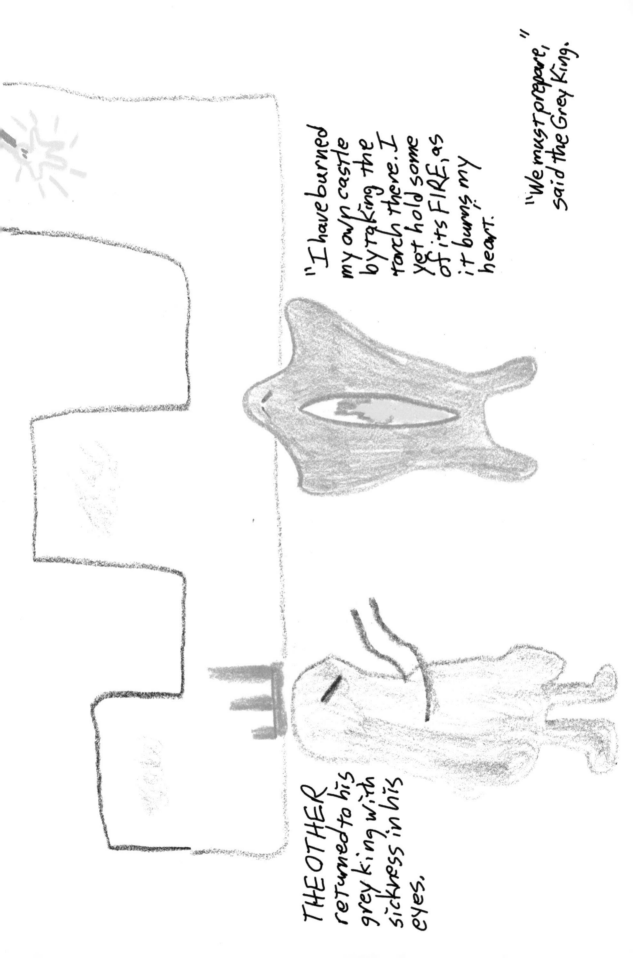

"I have burned my own castle by raking the torch there. I yet hold some of its FIRE, as it burns my heart."

"We must prepare," said the Grey King.

THE OTHER returned to his grey king with sickness in his eyes.

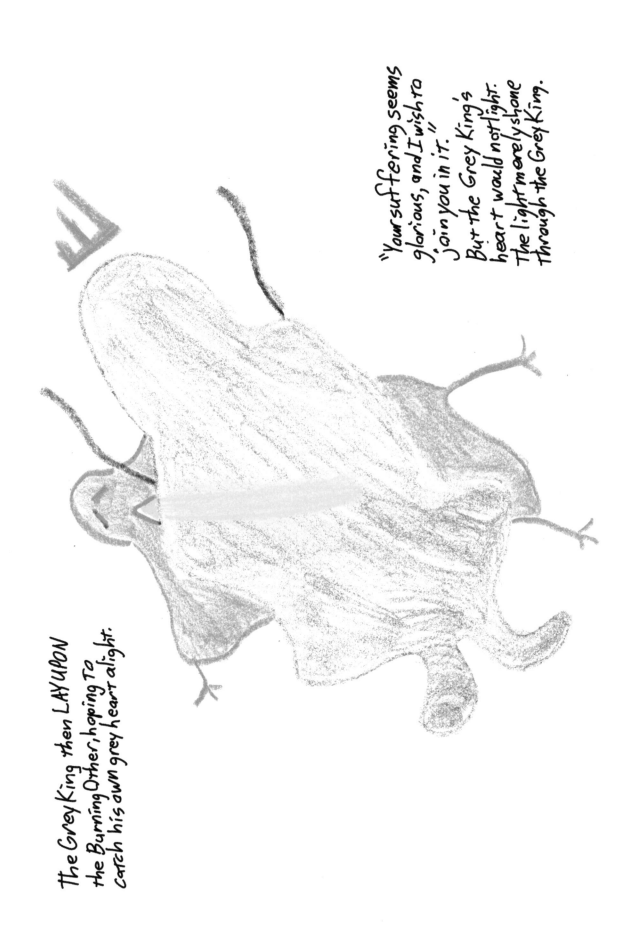

The Grey King then LAY UPON the Burning Other, hoping to catch his own grey heart alight.

"Your suffering seems glorious, and I wish to join you in it." But the Grey King's heart would not light. The light merely shone through the Grey King.

the Grey King CLAWED at the Other's heart, seeking clearance to enter.

Unseen and so close, The God's Lion weeps.

"I am not close enough to catch alight," moaned the Grey King. "I must, like the wick, immerse myself in the flame, so that I might BURN."

The Grey King's body became flame. His grey old body was now a black lump at the center. His grey eyes, too, remained. He took to his highest tower to wait for the embrace of the LION and his own ascendance.

The other Grey Kings took to their towers, hoping to at least bask in the reflected light.

The faces, the bodies were square. The castles were upside-down. Even the light was different. The lion could not be seen, not even a glimpse of his mane.

"Is this all there is?" cried the Grey King. "More? That's all?"

The square man demanded his name.

"I am a grey king."

After the square kings tore the blackness from his body, the grey king turned red, soaked in the blood he'd never had.

The God's Lion appeared to him.

"Why is there only more of this?" he pleaded.

I ASCENDED BY RITUAL, NOT CRUELTY, spake the Lion. FIND YOUR CROWN AND YOU SHALL BE MADE GREY AGAIN. TELL ME WHERE THE CROWN IS AND YOU SHALL RISE.

"Tell me!" begged the Grey King.
YOU STOOD SO HIGH THAT YOU LEFT YOUR WORLD. BUT YOU ARE NOT SO HIGH AS THE LION ASCENDANT. YOUR CROWN FELL OFF WHEN YOU VIOLATED YOUR OTHER.

LOOK AGAIN, said the Lion.
Indeed, the king was grey again.
THERE IS YOUR CROWN.
DO NOT FORGET THAT I
HAVE MADE YOU KING.
"I was ALWAYS
grey, ALWAYS the king!
The things you changed are
meaningless! Even the crown
does not matter!"
"Then I defy you!"
cried the Grey King.
"Now that I know where my
crown is, nothing can
stop me from
reclaiming
it!
For I am
King!"
FIND THE
ANIMAL, said the
Lion, disappearing into
the sun. YOU ARE READY.

"At last!" cried the Grey King. "A world with less!"

The Bird King, his head swimming after what he'd done to his Other, gazed upon the Grey King, half-visible in the air, with awe.

"The Grey God has come! Dim my light so that I might descend!"

"Take my hand, Bird King," said the Grey King. "To descend, you must first rise."

Anything said by a half-materialized greygod in the sky was good enough for the Bird King.

"Not as much as I have," said the Grey King. "Or you would have gotten here on your own."

"You're right!" cried the Bird King. "I have much to learn from you!"

"I am coming, Grey God! Oh, the things I have done just to gaze upon you!"

YOU HAVE DONE EXACTLY WHAT I WISHED, growled the Lion. YOU'D BE SURPRISED HOW MANY KINGS TAKE THE CRUELTY WARNING SERIOUSLY.

The Lion licked the last of God's blood from his paw.

COME ON UP.

"I have it, Lion of God!" cried the Grey King, holding aloft the Bird King's inner light. "I have been to all there is and taken so much fire and light that Night itself fears you!"

They swore they would never fall prey to such shabby metaphysical bunk like Up and Down.

"Not much of a king, really," sniffed one. "It takes more than a tall castle to be king."

"Still," said the other Grey King. "No reason not to renovate a little."

The other Grey Kings burned the castle of the departed, unwilling to be ensnared by its depravities. But also because it was the tallest.

After using up available resources to raise their castles very high, their value increased many times.

Although, the only possible buyer for a castle was the owner of the other one, and he would have to mortgage his castle to the other owner to raise the capital.

So they kept building, using pieces of the third, ruined castle.

With pieces of the departed king's castle built into their own, the two Grey Kings were able to open doors to other places. There they found an infinite supply of building materials.

True, these materials were the homes of other kings. But the two Grey Kings felt this was their right as discoverers.

The two Grey Kings looted the infinite worlds of their castles, building so high that even the mame of the LION could not reach the upper floors. The two Grey Kings now saw in full the doings of the LION and the mutilated body of GOD undying. They tut-tutted the LION and heard the groaning pleas of GOD only a little while as they built higher and higher.

Feasting on GOD's blood made the LION see himself as a god. But instead of doing as this god had done, the LION feasted all day and night on immortal, and therefore endless, blood. The LION was perturbed that the Grey Kings now stood in castles far above him. But it didn't bother him enough to stop drinking.

I AM NOW THE MAN OF THE GOD, was all the god would say as he wept and suffered.

At some point the wind would
have its say in this contest.
The castles lurched and bent
until they touched at the very top.

"Success!" cried one Grey King.
"I've doubled the value of my
home!"

"Disaster!" cried the other Grey King.
"We've built too high!"

The wind would prove only one
of them right.

In a moment, a Grey King went from doubling his home's value to having no home, no life, at all.

The wind continued its warning, shifting the remaining castle. "I am the tallest in the world," whispered the wind. "For I cannot fall."

The wind caught two birds with one stone, steering the falling castle onto the cloud where the LION fed. The wind was sick of the spectacle of the LION feeding on his old friend, GOD.

The one Grey King snapped up the crown left by the wind and went inside.

The One Grey King had never been inside any of the castles he used to expand his own. He'd always preferred to stand on top of each new one as it was raised into place.

He'd always seen it as one castle at a time when building. But, fleeing the summit of his desire for his very life, it just looked like too many stairs.

"Better hurry," chided the wind through the windows. "I might topple this abomination at any time."

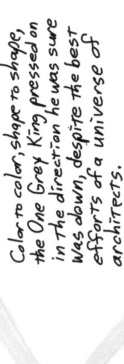

Color to color, shape to shape, the One Grey King pressed on in the direction he was sure was down, despite the best efforts of a universe of architects.

The wind tried to tell him he was going the wrong way, but even upside-down with a crown still resting on his head, the One Grey King knew the way down.

With a king's determination, the One Grey King passed down from castle to castle, through doors that didn't seem like doors so much as elaborate metaphysical dares.

He almost missed his own window. There'd been so many like it. The One Grey King barely heard the wind anymore. It may have been shouting, for all he knew. Still, the wind could bring the whole business down upon him at any time, so he dragged his tired self outside.

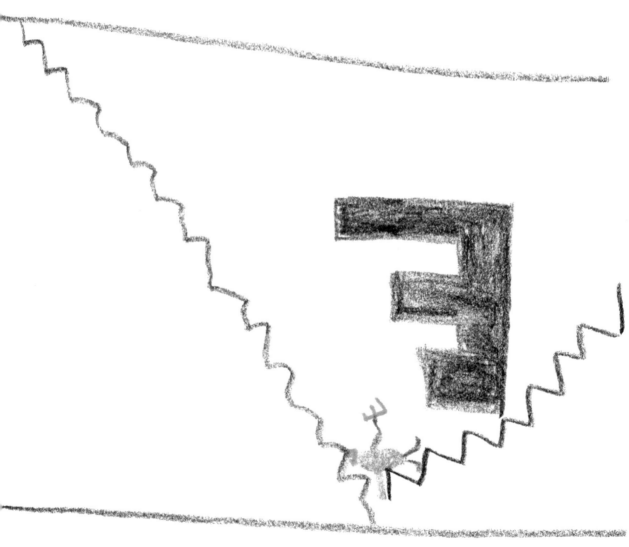

The wind still mocked the One Grey King.

"Just because you got out doesn't mean I can't destroy you. I can squash you like a bug with your own castle."

The One Grey King had an answer for the wind this time.

"You only have one building to drop on me. And if you miss, you are powerless to harm me."

"And what makes you think I'll miss?" asked the wind.

"We won't know until you do it. And in that moment, you are undone. Why not keep the power?"

The wind went silent. A comeback would take some time.

For a handshake and a spare crown, the KING BETWEEN was happy to take the other castles off the One Grey King's hands, as living in the space between everything and every other thing covers a lot of ground. Having castles between everything solved a lot of problems.

The wind gave up thinking about the people on the ground. It had a good comeback for the One Grey King, but lacking the tower to kill him took all the fun out of it.

And as GOD lay healing, he thanked the wind for its aid, and thought about what he would do once he was strong again.

Tomorrow, he thought. Tomorrow I'll destroy all the lions....

PHTHEOMANCY

is the art of prediction via patterns of decay of objects, like webs of sidewalk cracks, clusters of tire prints, constellations of shoe prints in snow. Learn how the collapsing world predicts the new! In this picture, you can see your future! If only you knew what it says. Find out before it's too late! Circle #190 on card.

RUSSIAN COMAS

Comas can be used to ride out all sorts of things! The DTs, depression, winter, all of it can be safely missed while in twilight sleep! We do all the work. All you have to do is sleep! Broke your pelvis? Sleep it off! Waiting for your wife to stop being mad at you? Sleep it off! Sad the last new show is over? Sleep it off!

CIRCLE #159 ON CARD

WHEN WAS THE RAPTURE?

THE CRUCIFIXION TOOK ALL THE GOOD AND PIOUS

THE RAPTURE WAS THE END OF THE CHRISTIAN WORLD

ALL THE SAINTS ARE TRIBULATION SAINTS

THE SEVENTH ANTICHRIST WILL BE THE TRUE CHRIST

THE BETRAYER AMONG THE ANTICHRISTS WILL SAVE US

FOR WE ARE THE UNREDEEMED, NOT THE DAMNED

ARE YOU THE SEVENTH ANTICHRIST?

BECAUSE YOU'RE A BIT LATE

YOU WERE SUPPOSED TO APPEAR IN 2016

BUT WE ALL KNOW WHAT HAPPENED THERE

YOU WERE SUPPOSED TO APPEAR IN 2016

YEAH, HA HA, FUNNY PERSON, NOT THAT GUY

SERIOUSLY, ARE YOU THE SEVENTH ANTICHRIST?

DO YOU KNOW WHERE HE MIGHT BE?

IF YOU KNOW HIM, PLEASE CONTACT ME

BECAUSE I'M ON A SCHEDULE HERE

IT CAN'T BE GOOD THAT HE'S LATE

CIRCLE #169 ON CARD

LOST?

You just need a little rewiring! Once your heart and omphalos are properly bridged, you can find your way out of any quandry! Build your moral compass out of materials in your own body!

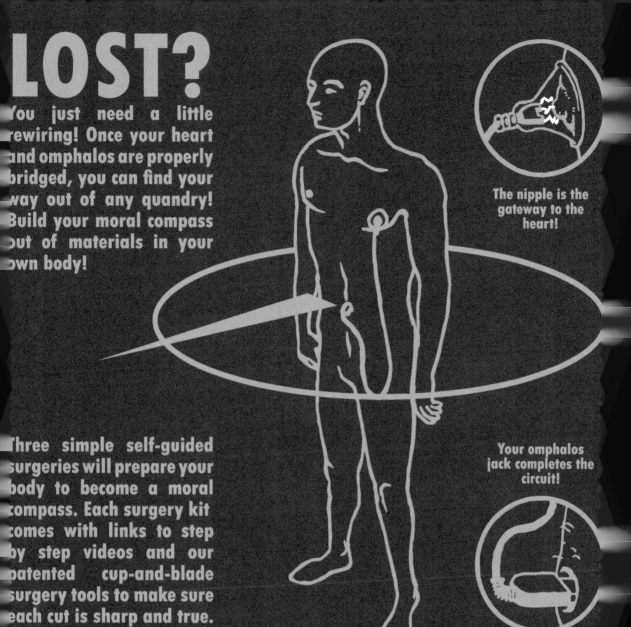

The nipple is the gateway to the heart!

Your omphalos jack completes the circuit!

Three simple self-guided surgeries will prepare your body to become a moral compass. Each surgery kit comes with links to step by step videos and our patented cup-and-blade surgery tools to make sure each cut is sharp and true. Modifying your nipple isn't for the faint of heart. But with cup-and-blade, you just press and twist to get the perfect incision. Your surgery kit also includes a bellybutton corer and splayer to make the port for your omphalos cable (sold separately). Once you're modified and plugged in, you're ready to follow the path to ultimate

What will you find when you become a living wayfinder for human improvement? You'll find opportunity! As a moral compass, you'll natually seek out other flesh that needs improvement. As a shining success story, you'll be able to share your story and this process! New converts will call on you locally to assist with their installations and upkeep. And every new convert means upgrades for you! It's time you leveled up. Send for our free kit today!

The following is a transcript of the June 12, 2020 episode of Ocean to Ocean FM. The show is absent from the OtO archive, but that's because Arlan Rutiger thinks guest hosts are noncanonical. Some of his fans have adorable theories about why this episode was "suppressed," but it's just that a substitute host opened the phone lines and got dogpiled. That's all there is to it. I regret nothing.—JIT

C. ANNE WELLS

is a free-lance writer and seeker of truth.

#108 on card

C. ANNE WELLS: Welcome back to the second hour of Ocean to Ocean FM. I'm C. Anne Wells, in for Arlan Rutiger. It's a beautiful evening here outside the oh to oh FM studio. In the station break I took a moment to step out and look at the stars, but now I'm back with all of you for another hour of parsing the unknown. As always, the second hour is brought to you by the fine folks at Ghoster. Ghoster—makers of the finest and most effective anti-tracking apps and software. Ghoster—they'll never see you going. This hour, I'd like to hear from the leaders without followers. Not every great idea finds its moment. Having a great idea doesn't build a movement. So I'd like to hear from you. The phone lines are open, our inbox awaits your missives. First call of the second hour of Ocean to Ocean is from Sacerdot, Arizona. Caller, you're alive on Ocean to Ocean FM. Speak freely but cleanly.

CALLER ONE: Um, hello.

C. ANNE WELLS: Hello, caller. Are you a leader without a flock?

CALLER ONE: I was just curious if Curtis Wolver was going to be on tonight.

C. ANNE WELLS: Curtis Wolver was scheduled for the second hour tonight but we had trouble getting a stable Skype connection via the router setup he required. We respect his desire to be undetectable to the mole people, especially since the blockbuster report from retired Col. Amy Davies featured on the January 20th show this year. With the possibility that the mole people have patched themselves into major underground telephone trunk wires, Mr. Wolver has every right to be concerned that the now largely untapped dial-up modem bandwidth has given the mole people a near-complete hold on 90s cyberspace. Incidentally, we do still have a few ReFax Kits on hand via our website o2oshow.co—remember that's co not com. ReFax Kits are plans and parts to modify your existing fax machine to detect phone data intrusion by anyone, be they mole people or...anyone. Let that idle fax time, not used sending or receiving, be used for knowing. Order now and get 10% off with the code KNOWING from now until the end of the broadcast. Caller, do you have one of these installed on your fax?

CALLER ONE: I'd prefer you didn't insult my intelligence. That ReFax Kit is junk! I fax a data cleaner sheet to number zero every day to scramble the mole people's surveillance. It works just as well, and you can use each sheet twice.

C. ANNE WELLS: Caller, I respect your dedication to thwarting the mole people. But may I respectfully suggest that faxing every day is time better spent bringing the fight to the mole people? With the ReFax Kit, you just install and forget.

CALLER ONE: It's junk!

C. ANNE WELLS: Agree to disagree, caller. Thanks for your input. Okay, new caller from Sea of Tranquility, Montana. You're on Ocean....

CALLER TWO: That's "Moon Terrae". Your state and region code choices are offensively limited.

[CROSSTALK]

C. ANNE WELLS: So, a caller from across the ocean of space.

CALLER TWO: Pfah! It's hardly a puddle of space. Your mind is too limited, C. Anne Wells!

C. ANNE WELLS: Are you a leader without followers, caller?

CALLER TWO: I am indeed between followers at the moment.

C. ANNE WELLS: Ah, between followers. So you have had some, and they...

CALLER TWO: Well, they left! Obviously.

C. ANNE WELLS: Now were these...locals?

CALLER TWO: Pfah! There are no indigenous life forms on the Moon! The Apollo mission ethnic cleansings saw to that.

C. ANNE WELLS: Ah, so you hold with Peyler, Deems, and others who believe that the moon rock samples returned to Earth by the Apollo missions were in fact key components in the Moon's natural oxygen geysers. You are an inhabitant of the post-paradise Moon.

CALLER TWO: Indeed I am. I have tapped into the Moon's oxygen core and have made room for ten to twelve young women to join me here in a new lunar paradise!

C. ANNE WELLS: Is your goal to repopulate the Moon?

CALLER TWO: No! The Moon's oxygen core will be depleted in a hundred years. And without the Moon's original inhabitants devouring rock and excreting breathable air, this place will become as dead as most earthbound believe it to be now.

C. ANNE WELLS: How can interested young women, I'm guessing between the ages of twenty-one and...

CALLER TWO: Sixteen.

C. ANNE WELLS: That's...less than twenty-one, caller.

CALLER TWO: I dunno. You sound nice. How old are you? I can cover relocation costs. Please, the Moon is so lonely! I don't even know why I came here!

C. ANNE WELLS: Caller three, from Coralville...Iowa.

JOHN IRA THOMAS: Hey there, Wells.

C. ANNE WELLS: Go...go ahead, caller.

JOHN IRA THOMAS: I gave you even odds to screen me or hang up when you saw the city.

C. ANNE WELLS: So, I am speaking with the JIT. Or the Anti-JIT?

JOHN IRA THOMAS: Well, that's a matter of context. But either way I am a leader without followers. You'd have to agree.

C. ANNE WELLS: For those listening: it's been a while since people have talked about the drawing of the young man who came to be known as the JIT.

JOHN IRA THOMAS: And later the Anti-JIT.

C. ANNE WELLS: Do you call yourself the Anti-JIT? That was a term previously applied to you by Whitney Allen Turner, who asserts that he is the JIT.

JOHN IRA THOMAS: Despite not having drawn the original picture. Despite not having written the words "The god of the king is going into the lion's body" on that picture. Despite not being me at all.

C. ANNE WELLS: Do his claims bother you?

JOHN IRA THOMAS: On the contrary. He might be making a liar out of me for calling tonight. The question I have for you is: what is a follower?

C. ANNE WELLS: An...adherent. A believer.

JOHN IRA THOMAS: A believer in the leader? A believer in a tenet of the leader? A believer in comfortable loosefitting clothing? The last caller, the statutory Moon rapist. How can we define a believer in him? What's that poor girl like?

C. ANNE WELLS: He didn't really get into his teachings.

JOHN IRA THOMAS: Well, to me he smacked of the charismatic. He admits there's a hundred years left on the Moon, so there's no future in it. But he's up there because he wants to be the cool guy on the Moon. He just wants people to accept him and all his pronouncements. Well, he wants girls to do that. But does that make him a leader? Or does that make him a follower of an imaginary bevy of adoring and unquestioning teenage girls with cab fare to the Moon? Which is the ideal and which is the real? Who's chasing whom? He's a real guy with imaginary qualities chasing completely imaginary beings that represent all he wants out of life. Now, I didn't call to punch down at this guy, except to say that I hope he doesn't live near a school.

C. ANNE WELLS: You want to question the nature and the relationship of leaders and followers. And engage in a little punching down to keep yourself amused.

JOHN IRA THOMAS: Find me someone who can punch up at that guy. Anyway, I think this is a worthy question. Can the unreal or supernatural be a follower of a real natural person? Isn't belief naturally tied to the non-tactile? Isn't that the only use for it? Belief fills in the gaps on the stuff we can't directly apprehend with the senses.

C. ANNE WELLS: I've been down this road with you before.

JOHN IRA THOMAS: Now you're exercising judgment? After dial-up mole man hackers and cheerleaders on the Moon? Are you looking for someone to believe in, or do you just want an entertaining hoax? Something untethered from reality so you can set it aside and tell people "you can't imagine I actually believed that, do you?" I submit that there are no more believers. There are only audiences. Shows that brand themselves as "reality" have audiences that simultaneously believe them to be real and a show. Or look at mass Christianity. The megachurches have pageants instead of preachers. The preacher is just a character in the church show.

C. ANNE WELLS: Some belief systems have been in practice for thousands of years. How does one generation's entertainment so successfully appeal to the next, if all religion is only a show? How do religions not get cancelled?

JOHN IRA THOMAS: Ohhh. Maybe religion as show is the newest incarnation of whatever it is that creates believers? Wells, you complete me.

C. ANNE WELLS: You do claim that you made me up.

JOHN IRA THOMAS: Hey, you came to that conclusion on your own.

C. ANNE WELLS: Which means that it's your claim, if I was made up by you. I won't say created. Stories can be made up out of words alone. A face can be made up by applying material illusions of color and shape. The idea of being made up can involve both the real and the unreal. Through my involvement in Jitting, you have made me up to be some kind of partner or arbiter.

JOHN IRA THOMAS: I can make up anything but followers. And so I am calling. You wanted leaders without followers, and here I am. You could have asked for time travelers or Orc kings or mole people to call in tonight. But in this hell of live radio, abandoned by your scheduled guest, you threw open the switchboard and practically asked for me and Whitney to call.

C. ANNE WELLS: You think Whitney Allen Turner will call?

JOHN IRA THOMAS: Scan your call list and see if Lamar, Colorado turns up.

C. ANNE WELLS: Why Lamar? Are you in contact with him? He despises you.

JOHN IRA THOMAS: Kinda, yeah. Kinda in contact, I mean. You might want to use a stronger term than "despises" now.

C. ANNE WELLS: A call from Lamar is holding. I will leave you on air if you promise not to turn this into a scrum. I will exact the same promise from Whitney. While I do that, we'll go to a station break. You're listening to Ocean to Ocean FM with C. Anne Wells, in for Arlan Rutiger.

[STATION BREAK]

C. ANNE WELLS: Welcome back to Ocean to Ocean FM. I'm your host, C. Anne Wells, in for Arlan Rutiger. This second hour is brought to you by Ghoster. Their suite of apps includes DisFriendigrator—the app that scrubs any unwanted bonds clean from all forms of social media. DisFriendigrator—unfriending that's easier done than said. We are back with the two most well-known figures in the Jitting movement. John Ira Thomas, also called the JIT.

WHITNEY ALLEN TURNER: Falsely.

C. ANNE WELLS: And Whitney Allen Turner, who is also known as the JIT.

JOHN IRA THOMAS: Only at his house.

WHITNEY ALLEN TURNER: You are the Anti-JIT! I am the true JIT!

JOHN IRA THOMAS: I love this part. Whitney, did you draw the picture?

WHITNEY ALLEN TURNER: I am the reason for the image.

JOHN IRA THOMAS: But who put the markers to paper that day?

WHITNEY ALLEN TURNER: The material aspects of the image are irrelevant. The image existed before you. Your feeble attempt to confine it to paper was the merest pinprick in the paper of the world.

C. ANNE WELLS: Gentlemen. This is your one warning.

JOHN IRA THOMAS: Whitney, I called in today because Wells here asked for leaders without followers. I'm one, and you are too. Which is weird, right? Because we're fighting over the same theological turf.

WHITNEY ALLEN TURNER: You don't want any theological turf, Anti-JIT. You want to burn it all away.

JOHN IRA THOMAS: Either way, we're duking it out over something imaginary. We're not fighting over money or a bowling trophy or anything we can put in our pocket. There are two of us. So who's the leader and who's the follower?

WHITNEY ALLEN TURNER: We are two leaders. And you can't put a bowling trophy in your pocket.

JOHN IRA THOMAS: Well, that's a waste of manpower. Even the people who wrote all those articles for *TIRE*, gassing about the aspects of the original drawing —they've moved on. They're writing mindfulness bullshit or selling Armageddon prepper kits or nutritional supplements made of penguin marrow. They can't remember what they spent their Jitting money on, it's been so long. We lost our moment. The audience went somewhere else.

C. ANNE WELLS: Whitney, my question for you is: if the drawing had not been drawn, would you have done any of this?

WHITNEY ALLEN TURNER: Of course! I am the JIT.

C. ANNE WELLS: But what form would the practice of this creed take? If the JIT is the one who drew the picture, who is the JIT if there is no picture? If there's no crucifixion, who is the Christ?

JOHN IRA THOMAS: I've been pelted with stuff for asking that one before.

WHITNEY ALLEN TURNER: To do battle with the Anti-JIT. Because the Anti-JIT does bedevil me! Has he told you what he's done to my magazine?

C. ANNE WELLS: Ah, so because you see yourself in a struggle with your opposite in terms of your creed, this makes you the JIT. The argument about drawing and not drawing the actual picture always seemed like a secondary argument to another, unstated one.

JOHN IRA THOMAS: Wait. So the ontology here amounts to our conflict being the sole animating force in our relative divinity? To argue makes us divine? I gotta say, I'm on board with that.

C. ANNE WELLS: But the disagreement itself—the JIT says you are not the JIT. Both of you claim that. You both claim the same thing, but mean different things by it. Your roles are defined by the argument and the argument does nothing to define you.

WHITNEY ALLEN TURNER: Trap! This is a trap. **[HANGS UP]**

JOHN IRA THOMAS: And Whitney has tapped out. He's so afraid of losing the last remnant of his belief system that he pulls the chute at the first sign that he might have to explain himself. "Thomas drew the drawing, but I am responsible for the picture." And there's no answer for the follow-up question.

C. ANNE WELLS: You say that you made me up. But I think we made you up.

You were just a child who crossed paths with someone who made you up to be an outsider art seer, an unwitting prophet. That person deified you in that moment, then stripped the divinity away to prevent anything else you might do from contradicting your moment of divinity.

JOHN IRA THOMAS: These kind of cons are always based on unrepeatable results. The best cons make it a selling point. How can we explain this unrepeatable thing? Send $19.95 for a 200 page attempt to do so. Faith in these things has always been about getting people to vote with money. I made money for somebody. You can't quantify faith in any other way besides cash money. Does the idea sell? How many units have you moved? Oh, not many, huh? Well, better luck with the next thing. If the truth doesn't sell, it's not the truth. We use this standard to judge a lot of things—art, books, movies....

C. ANNE WELLS: But there are exceptions. The so-called cult status achieved by works of art long after their creation comes to mind.

JOHN IRA THOMAS: A cult is a niche market, in those terms. We are surprised by *THE ROOM* because it suddenly started selling lots of tickets and discs. It didn't suddenly become good. *CITIZEN KANE* was always good, but it was a failure initially because it didn't sell tickets. And now it does. Maybe these things start with a critic who's pure of heart that persuades people to love something unloved. But that doesn't make something cult. Money changes hands. When something is much-loved and doesn't sell, we see it as a tragedy, an injustice. Why isn't love enough?

C. ANNE WELLS: I think love is enough to elevate art, though I'm not sure how this suddenly became about art. But perhaps this maps onto the discussion of religion. When something doesn't sell, we feel bad for the artist. If the artist is dead, I think we don't feel bad for anyone but perhaps the next generation who might not have access to that art. We feel bad that they aren't able to access and enjoy it.

JOHN IRA THOMAS: And that brings us around to the marketplace again. Access to art is related to its marketability. If we stick it on the Internet for free, it doesn't live forever. It gets taken and repurposed, even plagiarized. We like to think that means the artistic elements are then part of a larger system, making us all grow. But this system doesn't differentiate between art and crap. You'll find chunks of art in the Internet's stool right alongside genuine crap.

C. ANNE WELLS: I will wait patiently while you swing from nihilism to hope.

JOHN IRA THOMAS: It's not as easy as it used to be. Three years and change of irony blowouts and exploded norms have left creative minds spinning their tires. And, I would argue, religious minds as well. If religion is balm to a troubled soul, then it's time to get balmy. This is where the rubber meets the road. Does religion clear the lowest bar it sets for itself? Is it a comfort in troubled times? To bring things back around to my patch of phenomenology—does Jitting make anyone happy? Certainly not me, but I've long suspected I'm the one and only martyr Jitting has, or can have. I'm the only one who's suffered for Jitting.

C. ANNE WELLS: Certainly Whitney suffers.

JOHN IRA THOMAS: Only because I torture him. The Jitters ignored him. I was the only one to give him legitimacy.

C. ANNE WELLS: By denying him legitimacy.

JOHN IRA THOMAS: I used his name in a sentence, which is more than the other guys did for him. To them, he was another hand reaching for the Jitting dollars.

C. ANNE WELLS: They felt the same about you, at least the way you tell it. Every time you tried to cash in, you were denied. You've ascribed that to faithful souls who didn't want to hear a stray word that might deny your divinity, or agency of divinity. But if they are all charlatans, even you (if only by accident), then you are just another charlatan.

JOHN IRA THOMAS: I certainly felt like a sucker when I saw they were making money off of me. That's hardly a divine urge. Should I have gone to the temple and upset the moneylenders? I did that when I fired the *TIRE* staff.

C. ANNE WELLS: At Ruth Corley Watt's behest. Again, you were the vessel.

JOHN IRA THOMAS: Again? Oh, I'm the walkie talkie, right? I only have something of value to share when I let off the talk button so others can transmit through me. Why do people hate visible effort so much? People stole my hair. Did they make JIT wigs in the hope that the next lightning bolt from God swerves away from me and hits them? What was the divine part of Jitting? The picture itself isn't treated as a holy object. Competent attempts to recreate it are dismissed as chicanery. The words on the page aren't treated as holy text. Efforts to create more are dismissed as false. What is the holy element?

C. ANNE WELLS: It's faith. And faith can't be reasoned or explained.

JOHN IRA THOMAS: That's a dodge. That is my martyrdom in a nutshell. I'm responsible, but blind and handless. I drew the picture, but authorship is denied to me. If the picture wasn't special, there would be no question that a weird nine-year-old kid named John Ira Thomas drew that picture. But because it is special to someone else, they want to deny my authorship. Are they embarrassed that they respect the picture? Does that embarrassment force them to claim some ownership of the picture? Is all this Jitting business born out of a collective embarrassment at thinking the picture is special? They think their love and respect somehow mean that they participated in its creation or specialness. Do they wonder how art could possibly connect with someone unless the audience somehow participated in its creation? Wait. I think I just explained *STAR WARS*.

C. ANNE WELLS: Lamar, Colorado is holding again.

JOHN IRA THOMAS: It's your show.

C. ANNE WELLS: Whitney?

WHITNEY ALLEN TURNER: I am not embarrassed by the picture.

C. ANNE WELLS: Whitney. Whitney. You can remain on air if you answer my questions. If you hang up again, you're done for the night. Fair?

WHITNEY ALLEN TURNER: As long as it is your question and not the Anti-JIT's.

C. ANNE WELLS: I can't guarantee that he doesn't wonder the same thing that I do. What is your divine aspect? Not what makes you the JIT, or the artist, or even son of Ernie (which is by far your strangest claim). What makes you a spiritual leader?

WHITNEY ALLEN TURNER: Those are different questions.

C. ANNE WELLS: Formulate the question you think I am asking, then answer it. Not the question you want me to ask.

WHITNEY ALLEN TURNER: [sighs] Why...what...hm.

C. ANNE WELLS: Even if you might oversimplify it. Put it out there.

WHITNEY ALLEN TURNER: I am thinking!

JOHN IRA THOMAS: Thinking makes for bad radio, Whitney.

WHITNEY ALLEN TURNER: I am not going to do this if the Anti-JIT keeps interrupting me.

C. ANNE WELLS: Don't get distracted, Whitney. Just ask my question, as you understand it.

WHITNEY ALLEN TURNER: What...is...the undrawn picture?

C. ANNE WELLS: That's closer to the answer to my unasked question. My question is: what is the core belief of Jitting? And your answer is: the undrawn picture.

WHITNEY ALLEN TURNER: The undrawn picture is everything that the drawn picture is not. The drawn picture contains all of the flaws not present in the undrawn picture. That's important. Since the drawn picture possesses all of the flaws, all remaining qualities define the undrawn picture, thereby revealing it to us.

JOHN IRA THOMAS: My drawing was so bad, it sucked all ability to be confused about the nature of the divine into itself? Shouldn't it work like a filter, then? Shouldn't the drawn drawing, when held up to other things, reveal the divine nature of them?

WHITNEY ALLEN TURNER: No. It only reveals the qualities of the undrawn picture.

JOHN IRA THOMAS: So if someone made a chair that encompassed all the possible bad qualities of a chair, you'd know what a divine chair is. That's some Platonic bullshit.

WHITNEY ALLEN TURNER: There's no divine chair.

JOHN IRA THOMAS: How do you know? Have you seen the worst chair?

C. ANNE WELLS: What good is the undrawn picture, then? If it is the only divine thing...no divine chairs, no divine tables...then what good is it? Is the undrawn drawing all God has to share with us?

WHITNEY ALLEN TURNER: This...is...a...trap.

JOHN IRA THOMAS: Oh, Whitney. If you're gonna grit your teeth and try to stay on air, this is about to get really bad for you.

C. ANNE WELLS: You say you are the reason for the image. Is that the image on he drawn or the undrawn drawing?

WHITNEY ALLEN TURNER: There is no image on the undrawn drawing. It is undrawn.

JOHN IRA THOMAS: Now you're dodging. Another charismatic goofball. Whitney, there's a guy on the Moon who's totally up for this crap. Just buy a wig and tell him you're almost a junior. He'll send you a bus ticket.

[CROSSTALK]

JOHN IRA THOMAS: Fine, ok, fine. The reason I say that is this, then I'll back off it. Whitney talks like a follower but insists he's a leader. Whitney is chasing a phantom lunar cheerleading squad too. He's engaging in divination by questioning. He has no idea what he believes. Attention is divine to him. And when you ask him questions, he thinks he's accessing the divine instead of his subconscious. Nobody has devised a creed that works for him, so he surfs on ignorance and wonder. Those twin highs keep him arrested. Spiritually, he wants the first date to last forever.

C. ANNE WELLS: So Whitney hates leaders, and you hate followers. You build and smash creeds with zeal and velocity. You are without followers because you don't want any.

JOHN IRA THOMAS: All I ever wanted was an audience, not followers. Having followers has always felt unseemly.

C. ANNE WELLS: That's...all the time we have for this segment. I'm told the router issues have been resolved and Curtis Wolver is now holding. John, Whitney, JIT, Anti-JIT, thank you for your time.

WHITNEY ALLEN TURNER: Thank you.

JOHN IRA THOMAS: Mole people unite!

The COVID-19 vaccine is real, but it's not what you think. The answer isn't colloidal silver, or vitamin D, or keeping fabric off your face. The true vaccine has been hidden where no seeker would think to look—*inside the vaccine!*

Look, I'm no ordinary doctor. I have a Un.D. from Northwest Southeast Missouri State University. That's a doctorate in the universe. I've studied the biggest picture available to human minds, and I've got some news for you. The COVID-19 vaccine is the greatest trick perpetrated on mankind since space aliens or TV dinners.

The COVID-19 vaccine hides a dark secret, but it's not 5G human hotspots or recombinant gayness or lizard DNA. We should be so lucky to have lizard DNA! A deployable tail would have had us colonizing Mars by now.

Dr. R. Fussell
REINKIN

knows the secret of the shot is inside you.

#105 on card

Inside this trojan horse, this nefarious mark of Satan, is a secret nobody could have guessed, or even imagined. What I'm about to tell you is so far beyond the understanding of the most diligent citizen journalist or deep web researcher that they will call you a liar for even breathing it.

Inside this trick, this useless dram of saline, is the real vaccine. It's true! The dark forces of this world hid the protection against the novel coronavirus in the last place truth-seekers would look—*inside the fake vaccine!* Tell me you even suspected that one, and I'll mail you my Un.D. and you can put your name on it. I won't even stipulate trial by combat for it. It'll be all yours.

When you get the shot, the true vaccine will lie dormant in you. You just have to unlock the secret vaccine's power! This secret is FREE and can be applied at any time! You can get your shot months before you unlock the secret vaccine inside. And even if you get a regional vaccine variant that other forces may have tampered with, this secret can free you of those adulterations as well! All trackers will be dissolved by white blood cells. All genetic rewriting will be undone! Just get the government's "vaccine," send away for my unlocking information, and wait!

Won't the deep state be shocked to see you lining up for your shot! They think they'll have the last laugh, but you're already armed with the knowledge you need to get back to the world before. You'll be owning them at levels previously unimagined!

Why do you think the people in power who previously spoke out against the false vaccine went ahead and got their shot anyway? Because they know this truth! The difference is, I'm going to share that truth with you! So get your shot today! I'll show you how to make it work for real!

"Chevelations"

Circle #111 on card

The Southwest's
biggest religious
car and van art show!

Even if I weren't already baked into a cosmology followed by tens of people at its height, I'd have a hard time subscribing to any creed. I've never been much of a joiner. But in my travels, both physical and astral, I've run across only one person who seems to have an ontology and life plan that seems worth emulating.

The first transmission I saw from Camp Nature Boy was in the pile of ad submissions I sifted through in making the June 2000 issue of TIRE. The transmission resellers had included a VHS tape (a $29.95 value) to, I dunno, make the package more expensive to send. I slammed the tape home in the giant old RCA unit that I still regret not stealing from the TIRE offices.

LONZO

Lives at Camp Nature Boy, so you don't have to.

#121 on card

There was no introduction, no title card, no chyron. No attempt was made to alter the image in any way, except by committing it to magnetic tape. Lonzo, a solidly-built older man wearing what appeared to be a silver foil Christmas tree on his head, was seated at a kitchen table, holding a tiki head in one hand and a staff in the other. His voice was gruff. Each sentence seemed to spin up from deep within and gain volume and velocity by the end. There were long pauses that suggested he was listening to something and then responding. I later learned that this was due to the unique medium of communication to Camp Nature Boy.

Transmission into CNB contained no audio. Back when the tapes were made, the unseen questioner was tapping out questions in Morse code by making disturbances in a basic signal. It could have been a piece of metal tapping a plug connector, a half-unplugged signal unit being touched by a finger, something that disturbed the signal regularly. The signal was a video, so perhaps they used the very VCR that recorded Lonzo's responses to communicate with him. In between Lonzo's pronouncements, I could hear a lot of variable buzzing in what I assumed were the joined parts from edits.

I played the tape over and over on a couple of long nights at the little house on Corley Street. After a while, even the buzzing in the dark started to make a little sense. But even if I knew the means and the language, where would I transmit to? Using what signal? I wasted an entire night trying to figure out how to make contact with Camp Nature Boy.

I ended up tossing the tape into one of the many office piles I'd been making since the first day. How could I actually believe this stuff? I set my attention back to finding other ways to avoid responsibility for an entire issue of TIRE.

In 2015, a random neuron fired in my skull while fishing for online videos and I searched for Lonzo and Camp Nature Boy. He'd started uploading videos (or his mystery interlocutor had)! Here at last was a way to communicate with Lonzo!

I recorded a simple video of me asking him a few questions and stuck a link to it in the comment section below the newest of his videos. I was the only commenter. The next video uploaded was Lonzo intoning "You look like a fish and make the same amount of sense!" Apparently sound still didn't make the jump to wherever Camp Nature Boy lay.

In making contact with Lonzo myself, transmitting my own image with questions drawn on paper worked well enough. Nowadays, I use PowerPoint on a tablet. Occasionally I have to flush the gate, a process only cursorily described to me by Lonzo. Basically, it's a frequency spike that makes my gums ache.

All communication with Camp Nature Boy is at best cursory. Lonzo's ability to see me depends on the video looking like it's from the VHS era. Apparently most of the Internet is not visible to him.

He'd found YouTube via uploaded vintage videos and is able to keep a tenuous connection to our reality through it. Flushing the gate has gotten harder and harder. I may end up looking like Max Headroom before it's over.

What follows is an interview conducted over six weeks of trading videos and flushing the gate repeatedly.—JIT

JIT: Does the hat protect you or project you?

LONZO: The hat is an antenna which helps me focus and send transmissions beyond the fence.

JIT: What's the purpose of the transmissions?

LONZO: I must keep in contact with the outside to keep the supplies that we depend on for survival. Otherwise we would need to do some type of work.

JIT: How are supplies getting through?

LONZO: UPS. Utopian Postal Supply and Plumbing.

JIT: Has Camp Nature Boy always been there, or did you build it?

LONZO: We moved in after the Boy Scouts left and didn't come back.

JIT: How did you get to Camp Nature Boy?

LONZO: Turned left at the Duds and Suds then it all got kinda hazy.

JIT: How big is the pocket of space where you are? Do you have neighbors? Is the Duds and Suds still visible to you?

LONZO: Only them critters outside the fence. Got no idea about what's beyond the woods.

JIT: Would you consider returning to our reality?

LONZO: Maybe for a visit to Branson. We have wore out that Yakoff record.

JIT: Are you well? Have the originals advanced beyond the omphalos into the edge of vision?

LONZO: Got a rash that won't go away. We outgrew our shiny suits.

JIT: Does the roar of a gorignak make you feel like you lost your car keys?

LONZO: Nah them's good eating. Send more BBQ sauce.

JIT: Are there traces of bleed back into Camp Nature Boy? Do things seem more real there, even if only in fits and starts? Will wearing a hat help?

LONZO: I never take it off.

JIT: Do you have any questions for us?

LONZO: Did Gilligan ever get off the island?

JIT: Briefly. They almost took the Harlem Globetrotters down with them. Or the smoke monster got him.

LONZO: Great shakes.

JIT: Reality isn't too stable here, either. Cough syrup remains legal, so there's always hope.

LONZO: We never get sick here. No germs. I haven't had a booger since we got here. Not even sure how long we been here. The days are wacky. One day here is three months there.

JIT: The gate between our realities does have its surprises. The last BBQ sauce delivery, I nearly fell out of the transition field because I thought I smelled purple. But I realized it might be my fault, since whoever smelt it dealt it.

LONZO: Oh no. Tonight we are having potted meat and kim chee.

JIT: That fits.

LONZO: We had q-tip and gravy fondue last feeding time.

JIT: Do you have any advice for us?

LONZO: Yes. Plant your corn early and use deodorant sparingly. Brush your teeth with ketchup.

I am only troubled slightly by notions of who or what rejects digital signals to Camp Nature Boy. What strips out or masks the audio of signals coming in? Why does making the content of a digital signal look analog fool this unknown gatekeeper?

I never did try to contact the seller of the original VHS tapes to see what they knew about the signal issues. And that's because, and I cannot stress this enough about all the TIRE advertisers, fuck those people. They worship and believe in the money you send them, nothing more. Lonzo would feed any money he somehow received to the barking oysters along the Blue Western Whorl of Camp Nature Boy. He has no need of it.

I hear the tut-tut of the sagacious reader and know they think "This Lonzo is messing with you." Is Lonzo different than any other entity promising wisdom, happiness, and salvation in this respect? Are they not all weirdly selective in their communications, either by design or choice? Why is that a disqualifier to wisdom?—JIT

MILK

does not spoil! A spoilant is introduced in the "pasteurization" process to keep us from living eternal lives. Milk is and has always been the food of the gods. The creation of milk is a holy act, made divine by the sacrifice of cows. The dairy barons have known this since the nineteenth century, when the first mass cattle sacrifices began. Beef is not good for us, yet it has been forced down our throats for generations. It's all part of the dairy barons' efforts to live forever! They keep the pure milk to themselves, imbuing it with power by mass cattle sacrifice. For the rest of us, they unlock a spoiling agent with heat, a process developed by Louis Pasteur, who died only four years ago! He passed these secrets on to me on his funeral pyre to share with the world! The burden of this world had become too much for him to bear. Shouldn't we have a chance to live forever? Why should we clean up after mass ritual sacrifice by eating the victims? We must take the power away from the dairy barons! Find out what you can do to live longer today!

Circle #138 on card

Nutrition Facts

0 servings per container

Serving size 0 cup (0mL)

Cattle souls per serving

1508

	% Daily Value
Karmic Cost	-39%
Purgatory Time	+6%
Kantian Ethics	0%
Hinduism	-100%
Good Place	-76.4%
Sodium	5%
Cholesterol	8%
Dietary Fiber	0%
Sugar	0%
Protein	16%

Warning: doing nothing to stop all this exacts a cost on your soul and will hamper post-life options. Values are based on an average life with basic valuation of life, happiness, and property. Virtue ethics may skew some numbers depending on the virtue extolled. If you wish to forego any influence on post-life options and drink unpasteurized milk with a genocidal chaser, aka the vampire option, these values are null and void.

When I jitted again for *TIRE June 2000*, I thought for sure I was done. I'd drawn every last thing I could with crayons, and further attempts were repetitive and derivative. And I thought: "What am I—the JIT or the Jitters?" Then the coronavirus turned us all into homebodies.

I had gathered a cache of varied art supplies over the years, just to see if any of it would provoke some more Jitting. Previous experiments hadn't amounted to much, and returning to crayons only went so far. But when I started playing with an eight color Crayola watercolor set, I managed to do two things—tap into a new medium and provoke my artist friends to intervene.

The artists I work with at Candle Light Press are the greatest. And they all believe that anyone can make art. Originally, I tried to enlist one of them to draw *MEGACONTEMPLATIONS* based on my drawings. They all said this was something I needed to do myself. And they were right. Plus, who wants to get sucked into the whole Jitter culture?

When my friends say anyone can make art, they mean everyone has something to say and some means to say it. It's not necessarily refined or even good. But it is art when you say it with pictures.

When I showed my fledgling watercolor efforts to Jeremy Smith, he decided I could use a few lessons. He armed me with the tools I needed to work at my level, and he made the most important change—my brushes.

I think that was the camel hair that broke the camel's back, so to speak. Later, I learned all the artists were thinking about that crappy Crayola brush and wincing. Everyone can do art, but get the right tool for the job.

So I started painting at my desk, snapping pics as I went along and sending them to Jeremy. And he'd nudge me along by showing me a new technique, like burning. Burning is great. You wet finished paint to dilute the color or push it out of the way to put in a new color. It's great for lightning.

Suddenly I was cranking out a painting a day. I was Jitting again. So here are the results of that entire process, from the last of the crayon to watercolors and beyond. It appears there is no end to the Jitting.

But that's how I am. I write everything like it's the last story I'm telling with those characters. Then when people ask me if there's going to be another one, I always say "No, I can't imagine how that story could go on." And then, a week later, I do know.

So I am done saying there will be no more Jitting. I'll have to torture the Jitters some other way. But I can't imagine how the torture could go on. Oh wait….

THE JIT

is mixing media now, so all bets are off.

#143 on card

Long after the world had passed to dust, the living image of it remained on God's eye.

Only God on his
cloud remained
in the Void.
Where the world
would have been
was marked only
by God's gaze.

The image of the world was perfect
(for it was God's own eye, after all).
The image of the departed world
seemed to deny the reality of the
stars that remained.

The Void at once sought to claim God, yet respected his existence. After all, in the beginning there had only been the two of them. And the Void believed in sticking with the one who brung you.

But God and the Void were hardly alone.

For in that perfect image of the departed world on God's eye was the mudman. God could not let the mudman escape his gaze, even if the mudman had attempted to escape by ceasing to exist. God would not be fooled by such a shabby trick.

The half OTHERS may not have been exactly as they were, but it's God's memory that counts and this is how they are now. There was no pesty reality to contradict him.

And with this
realization
came relief,
then joy,
then an air-
shattering
burst of
lightning.
It was settled.
There was only
one god, and
no one left
to claim
otherwise.

At some remove, a sterner, more rule-oriented god could only wonder how all that took so long. He was unable to see the other god, as gods are uncomfortable with the idea of peers. The god he observed was a powerful hole in the air, like the eye of a hurricane.

This god's own world had long been a wasteland, rendered lifeless in a war between every cell of life that lived on it. This other god mostly spent time tidying it up. This god would make great perfect cubes of ocean water, only to lose them whenever his attention returned to the task.

"Is this what they felt, thinking of me?"

There was a mountain in this world with one perfect smooth side. This god didn't create it. It was just... there. This god would come in close, nearly touching the ground, just to look up at it.

This was a rule-oriented god. To worship this god, one had to follow the rules, any rules.

But this god had never bothered to communicate or create any. The smoothness of the mountain beckoned the touch of power.

In an unguarded moment, this god wrote the first divine rule:

THOU SHA.

(The divine text is familiar to you because you are observing this from my remove.)

It was a good start, but the will just fell away. The first rule could go either way. Not even to THOU SHALT. This god considered finishing the thought, but decided it would keep until life farmed.

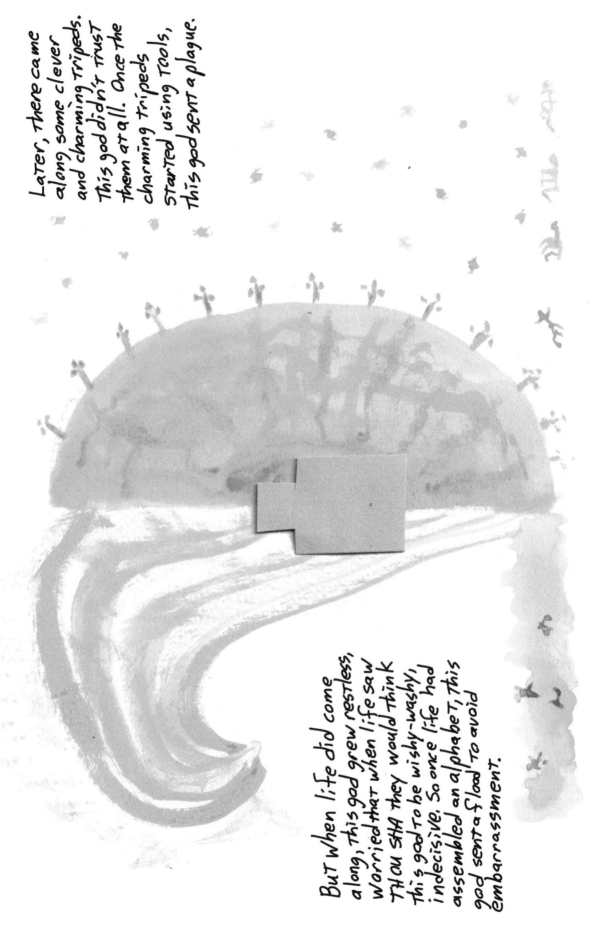

Later, there came along some clever and charming tripeds. This god didn't trust them at all. Once the charming tripeds started using tools, this god sent a plague.

But when life did come along, this god grew restless, worried that when life saw how SHA they would think this god to be wishy-washy, indecisive. So once life had assembled an alphabet, this god sent a flood to avoid embarrassment.

Even after flooding the world, this god was stuck seeing THOUSHA. Then along came some very sharp cephalopods, and by then this god was over it. This god constructed a cloud, the only one in the sky. And in it, this god slept.

On awakening, this god found a thriving and clever cephalopod culture living under the sea. And their god was a cloud, a tantalizing unique entity outside their atmosphere. And their name for their god was Thousha.

JTT

Meanwhile, at some remove, a cruel god watched with disdain, wondering how all this could take so long...

This god was furious. How clever could these cephalopods be, if they thought a bed was their god! But lightning couldn't reach them and flooding was pointless.

So is the crueler god observing us from a remove, both artist and reader?

Does this crueler god dream of a simple brutal resolution for us?

We can see the crueler god from the safety of our remove.

How many humans do we know think they too watch us from a remove?

Since the time of Democritus, humankind has carried the bias of the big. We talk of big things as if they are made of smaller helper parts that join forces to make big things. But physics increasingly shows that big things are side effects of the real business of extremely tiny things that have no more idea of us than the meal that created a specific fart.

We assume that the smallest part of a thing somehow retains the properties of that thing. I think it's a religious holdover, assuming small things only have a purpose in making big things. But human life, all life, is a side effect.

We have a broad and mysterious effect on particles. We are their gods. Gods are a side effect of human activity. We are made of particles, but they do not create us. Like gods, we are a side effect of the activity of smaller beings.

Jillane Sif
HENFORSAKER

is ready to talk about the very small things.

#183 on card

We are the astrology of quarks. Our behavior relates to quantum particles in the same way the position of stars affects us. We are their deities, going about our primarily amoral business while quarks and muons continue to be rocks and air. Occasionally we smash a few atoms and supercollide a particle to keep them on their toes.

Is a supercollider so different from one of Apollo's arrows? Is an atomic blast not a plague, a chain reaction of death? It has to be asked: are we benevolent gods? Is science a death cult that has sacrificed particles for reasons unfathomable to them?

It is easy to cast science in the role of the quantum Satan. But we affect the quantum scale in everything we do. We still do not understand most of what goes on beneath our sight. Gods create humans and promptly lose control of them in mythology and religion. At best they cajole, tempt, and violate them, but they never control them.

We did not create the quantum world, but we have been born to affect it in subtle and profound ways. We did not choose this work. It chose us. And that work is to set in motion the quantum eschaton.

We can remake reality by convincing the particles that their gods are angry with them. And when gods do not directly speak through prophet or angel, they speak in fire and death. This is where you come in!

I have made arrangements with an institute in Novosibirsk, Russia to produce random extra firings of their collider. Even scientists have to eat, and for cash money they will start particle Ragnarok for us! To them, particles are even less aware than the rabbits they test mascara on! They're totally on board!

Once the particles are convinced that the gods are angry, they will reorganize. And our world will materially change. Come change the world with me!

My moment of epiphany was outside a HyVee four years ago. I saw a sign that said *can redemption* and a door opened in my mind. Clear as day, I saw the words *find me here* below it. HyVee had asked half a question, and my mind finished that question. Now it's time for an answer. I did my part. So you need to provide the answer. *Can redemption find me here?* Please tell me. I tried HyVee. They have no idea what I'm talking about. I've tried to get them to run a version of this ad in their magazine, but they won't respond to me. It's irresponsible to open the door in someone's mind and let it just sit there. Light and inspiration flooded in initially, but now it's just letting in flies. Something needs to pass through the door or it needs to be closed. I've tried forgetting about the revelation, but that's not how revelation works. Once it happens, you are changed. The question burns in my mind, and spawns others. Can redemption *only* find me here? Can redemption find *only* me here? Can redemption find me *only* here? When did *only* get into the mix? I've stared at that sign for hours, and all I get is *can redemption find me here?* It's infuriating.

I mean, what business does HyVee have putting up signs like that? What other epiphanic triggers await me in there? I've never had a life-changing moment at a Fareway. What are they doing right? Have you had a moment at an Albertson's, or a Publix, or a Whole Foods? A Piggly Wiggly? I need to know the answer to this question. Do you have it? I am a seeker looking for answers, and there is no society, no religion, no sect, no cult that has answered this question for me. I've traded time, money, blood, and four iterations of my transmortal soul to those who claimed to have answers. But they all have their own axes to grind. We live in an age where no idea is too strange or unique to not be expressed. Why not this idea? I have tried to find it myself, but have come up empty. Are you looking to build a sect, a cult, a dungeon family? I will be your first, best adherent if you can answer this question. Cult member seeks cult leader. *If you can crack this problem, you can be a cult leader!* Have you ever wanted to start a compound? I'm your guy! Answer my question and I'm all yours! HyVee's loss
is your gain! Circle #136 on card.
Act now!

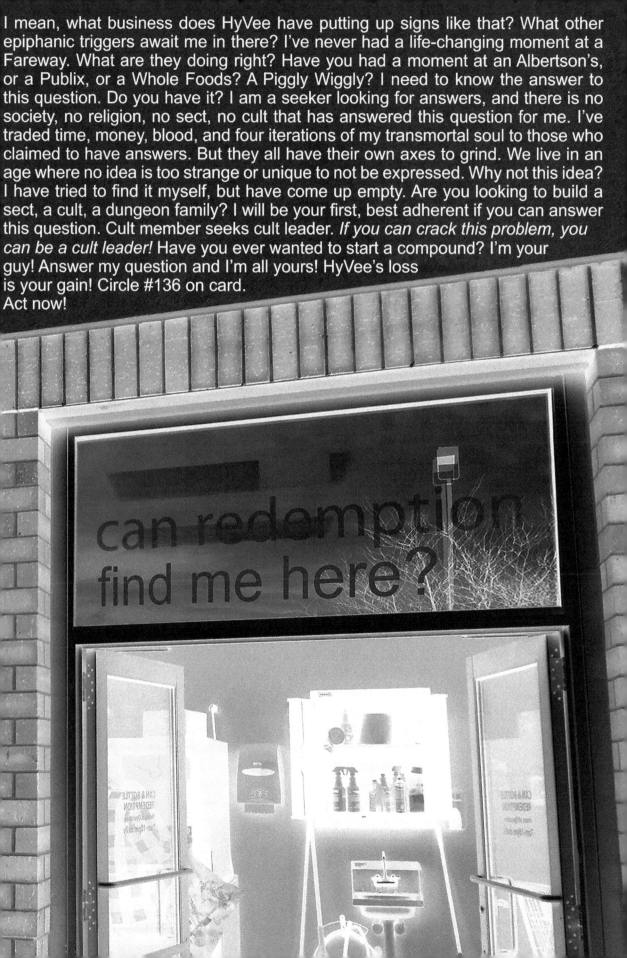

I love Bible tracts, the jankier the better. Chick tracts are the Pokemon of tracts, and tracking them down is fun. But give me a homemade tract and I'm up on a cloud. Working in and near a major hospital for a couple decades has enabled me and friends wise to my interests to collect a wide variety of bespoke visions of Christianity passing as mainstream.

People who visit hospitals often seem to have a special urge to express their theology. They're usually homebound to begin with and the hospital is where they get to see and meet new people. So whenever I pass through a patient area I keep my eyes open for tracts. The beginners place them with the magazines. The real pros know to casually place the tract on a seat or on the floor, just peeking out from under a chair.

I've even used the format to sell my graphic novels. Possibly the rarest JIT ephemera are the three Jesus fives I made in the early aughts and dropped on the floor of the Wizard World Chicago convention. A Jesus five looks like a real five dollar bill folded in quarters. When you pick it up and unfold it, it's only half the width of a five. And in the center it says something like "Disappointed? Come to Jesus and you won't be!" And then there's a church address or something. I made mine a $5 off coupon for my book *NUMBERS*. It had our table number on it so they could find us. I dropped one each day of the convention and never saw them again. Oh well.

THE JIT

wants a moment to talk to you about lions.

#149 on card

Sadly, homebrew tracts have faded with the advent of social media. People just post their crazy now. There's no craft in reposting a meme about Adam and Steve. Liking things has never seemed so negative as it does today.

I do still see tracts at truck stops. They're pretty cookie-cutter, except for the Chick tracts. Jack Chick may be dead, but his madness lives on.

There are lots of tract websites now that will print your church info on the back of a stock photo gangbang with pithy Bible quotes, aping the business model that made Jack Chick the world's most published comics writer. These new tracts are printed on glossy stock and sit on the rack next to the papers with ads placed by newly-minted pyramid builders and people who just need a steering wheel for a '73 Dodge Dart. Can you help a brother out?

So here's my tract. Look for it at truckstops or hospital waiting rooms near you. This will replace *MEGACONTEMPLATIONS* as my go-to for warding off street preachers and Gideons. Because nothing scares them off faster than whipping out your own tract and saying "I'll take your tract if you take mine." They are not ready for that shit at all.

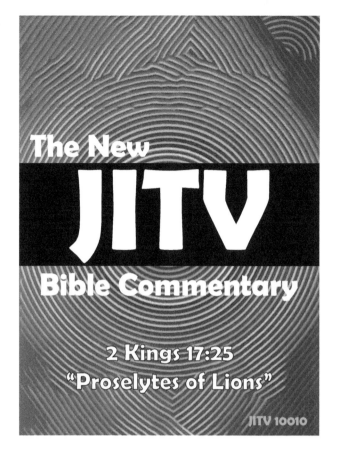

The New

JITV

Bible Commentary

2 Kings 17:25
"Proselytes of Lions"

JITV 10010

There are times when God wants to kill us with lions. It happens more often than you think. Have you ever walked into a room and thought *why couldn't there be a lion here right now?* That feeling is God.

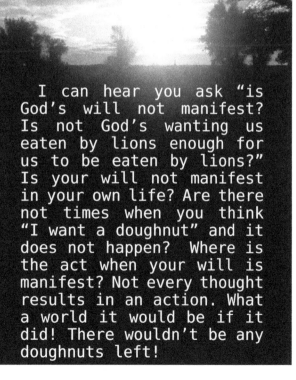

I can hear you ask "is God's will not manifest? Is not God's wanting us eaten by lions enough for us to be eaten by lions?" Is your will not manifest in your own life? Are there not times when you think "I want a doughnut" and it does not happen? Where is the act when your will is manifest? Not every thought results in an action. What a world it would be if it did! There wouldn't be any doughnuts left!

So ask yourself, wherever you go — why are there no lions here? Were there lions that God took away to save me? Are there lions on the way because God is displeased with me, or with someone who was just here? What if I meet God's lions, and they're on their way to the person God is mad at? Are they going to care? Have they traveled so far that they have to eat and I have to be consumed by lions to fulfill God's will for someone else?

When there are no lions, it means something. There are no accidents in God's creation. You have to find out if God is unhappy with you, because the lions could be on their way. And even if they don't find you, they might find someone you love. Lions are not precision weapons. The Romans tried mounting them for their cavalry, and they got eaten. They started riding horses and everything worked out. And you can be sure God will not send a horse to eat you!

God sent lions to eat the Samarians because He was angry with them. They didn't make God angry enough to send a plague, or fire, or locusts, or crib death, or any of the classic punishments. God was only sort of angry. He wanted the punishment to be a little miraculous— lions didn't really live in Samaria. It had to be something that wouldn't be mistaken for bad luck or poorly-stored garbage. Those lions showed up to say *this is God's will! Why else would we be here?*

Another point to consider is—why lions? Are the lions themselves being punished, tasked to leave their homes (perhaps even inadvertently starting power struggles within their prides) and walk miles upon miles? Or is it a lion pilgrimage? A lion crusade? Are lions worshipping God? When God sends a man, He can give a direct order, or He can send signs for the man to interpret as the will of God. Is it the same with lions? We know of no scriptural basis for God mind-controlling anyone or anything. So He must seek the worship of the lions. And lo, the lions responded!

The locusts worship. The frogs do not worship, for they were carried by a great wind. This proves that amphibians are incapable of ascertaining the will of God. Only mammals and insects seem capable of this.

What, then, can we make of the scripture of lions? Do they share this story of the crusade to Samaria to liberate it of syncretic Christianity? Do they possess the true method of worship? They seem to know it when they don't see it.

Lions communicate, because they have a social order. A rogue male does not know to leave when encountering another's pride. He is told to leave with roars, scents, and blood. Lions communicate.

Is, then, the carcass of a gazelle the writing of a lion? Is each tear and rend of the flesh a text from the beings whom God trusts to send His message? Just as we cannot read the writing of angels, we cannot read the scripture of lions. We can debate whether an angel wrote some text or not, but there is no question of the lion's authorship when we see its work.

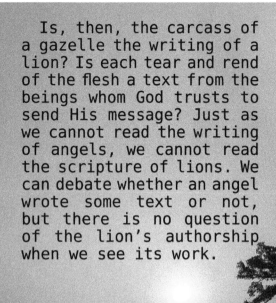

And can we not hear the fury of God in the lion's roar? A lion's tongue is itself a fearsome tool. It can lick the skin off a man so that it may drink his blood.

In 1898, two lions brought the building of a railroad to a complete halt for nine months in a place called Tsavo. Newspaper accounts described the fate of the workers as like the Samaritans devoured in 2 Kings. What was the scripture of the Ghost and the Darkness? What divine knowledge was inscribed in those men? Why was it so important that the lions trapped hundreds of men for months, just to make them understand?

Those lions were determined to tell us something we shall never know. In their lair, Patterson found a vast array of bones. In these, too, are the lions' scripture.

How do we know that God's Word is in the rent flesh and sinew of man? What is the advice they give for when a lion charges? Stand your ground. Don't run. If you run, you will definitely die. But a charging lion may just be warning you, experts say. If you show fear, the lion will claim you. God has decreed that we must be judged by the lion. God and the lions abhor a coward. Would God not make it our decision, if this world and its beasts are man's to use? But with lions, it is different.

Psalm 104:21 *The lions roar for their prey and seek their food from God.* It's God's call whether you are food, free, or a lion's journal. The lion knows. And it will tell you.

But perhaps the lions are being punished. Imagine knowing God's will and not being able to communicate it with another species! You know this feeling. How sad is it that your dog or cat will never know God's Word?

In Greek myth, Cassandra saw blood everywhere, but none of her captors knew or cared to learn her language. And so there was blood. So the lion is burdened with great knowledge that it cannot share. There is no lion heaven. The knowledge does not help them. It can only help the screaming sacks of meat and blood that can't remember if you're supposed to make yourself big like a bear when confronted. No wonder lions are so ill-tempered!

And what was the lions' sin? What did they do to deserve such torment? Why is their life a hell on earth? They are the souls of men who existed before the Word of God was made manifest on earth! There is no place in Heaven or Hell for these poor souls.

Now given the word of God, they have a mouth which cannot preach; paws which cannot write in any language of man; a countenance that inspires fear, not love. They want to share it, but cannot. Now they are hunted to extinction by rich half-wits who shoot them from Range Rovers and pose with their carcass as if it were an achievement and not a package tour feature.

So where do these souls go, now that the lion is almost gone from the earth? What animal now carries the burden of the unsaved cavemen? No animal at all!

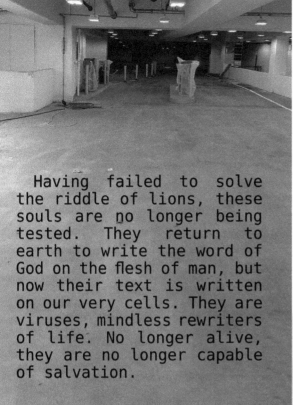

Having failed to solve the riddle of lions, these souls are no longer being tested. They return to earth to write the word of God on the flesh of man, but now their text is written on our very cells. They are viruses, mindless rewriters of life. No longer alive, they are no longer capable of salvation.

They now only write the Word, lacking any capacity to understand the irony they felt as lions. The viral soul only feels God's purpose, writes only His Word. They are as free as they will ever be, for God's mercy is infinite. They will still never know heaven, since they failed the riddle of lions.

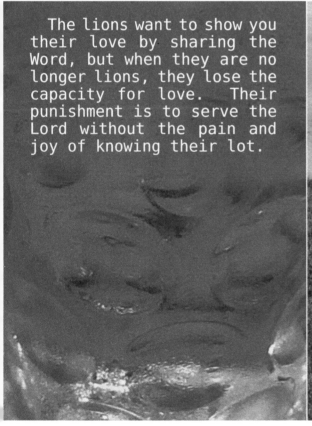

The lions want to show you their love by sharing the Word, but when they are no longer lions, they lose the capacity for love. Their punishment is to serve the Lord without the pain and joy of knowing their lot.

And now you know that God has posed the riddle of viruses to you. Now you know that God is using the souls of pre-Christians to tell you something.

Will you listen?

Will you understand?

Listen.

God is roaring!

Hear Him!

There are times when God wants to kill us with lions.

The next stage of yogic perfection currently eludes us. Even our greatest yogis admit that the next stage may well be inspirational or even purely accidental. While they try minute changes in the finest points, I'm asking you to help with the bigger picture.

My mother, Yogini Becca Hartley-Stevens, left me with the Yoga With Becca mail order business in 2016 when she accepted a position at the FDA that makes sure vitamins are never analyzed or tested for efficacy. It's a very important job.

I was left with a small yoga empire and not a clue what to do with it. I have a forestry degree and a name that means "turtle." I'm not equipped for this.

I had to end the TV show, because hiring someone is all headaches and overhead and I can't touch my toes. The clothing line was wholly inadequate in the face of the lululemon juggernaut. The only assets available that are worth selling are the books.

The books are actually really interesting, complex reading. Mom studied with several yoga masters and, going strictly by the variety in handwriting in the manuscripts, got them to write most of them.

Using these manuscripts, I commissioned a series of yogic manuals with the greatest care, to preserve the knowledge within. The people I paid to do this didn't do an awesome job, unfortunately. The warehouse of books that represents my entire fiscal future on this planet is full to the top with volumes that have misprinted pages, editorial problems somehow introduced during printing, and pages with profane messages drawn undoubtedly by the printers themselves.

But there is a lesson here. No consequence is final, save death. What can I do with a stockpile of incorrect yoga manuals? I can make yoga better! And you can help!

OUR LOSS IS YOGA'S GAIN! In following these divergent intellectual paths, we may yet discover the next level! Simply choose a volume that would be your next level and follow it as if it were true! All the other yogis and yoginis are busy following the rules and training and bending the way others have for centuries. You can break new ground!

How is yogic research done? By trying new things and seeing if you transcend! You can't just try random things. That would take forever. I choose to believe the flaws in these books point the way to new knowledge!

YOU COULD BE THE FIRST TO ASCEND NEXT! I may have ruined my mother's legacy, but my failure is your great opportunity to ascend!

Kurmasana STEVENS

is so wrong he's right again.

#152 on card

CRYSTAL MASKING

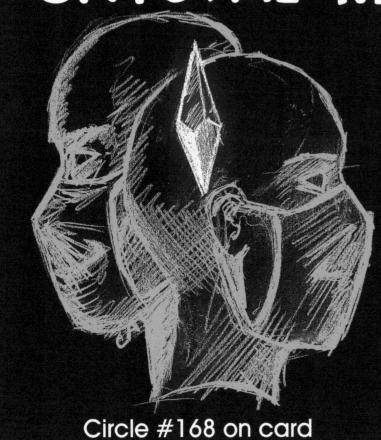

Tired of having to schedule floor time to have crystals on your face? Sick of skin glues that promise crystal adhesion but fail the first time you smile or sweat? Wear your crystals discreetly and channel more of their power! Keep your anti-COVID crystal cures close to your face and absorb more of their energy! Better than keeping them in your pocket! Safer than keeping them in your mouth! Even better—it's cleverly disguised as a surgical mask, allowing you the power of your cure while avoiding conflict with people who think the mask alone confers protection. Twelve crystal pockets line the inside, allowing you to maximize your crystal contact time! All they'll see is a mask, but you know better! Let them think you're playing along! You'll have the last laugh!

Circle #168 on card

STOP ACTING LIKE YOU KNOW BETTER

Facts just don't prove anything anymore. If they did, we'd all agree on everything! So what are you to do when someone you care about has fallen prey to some liberal conspiracy? Facts are useless. Argument is just rhetoric. Posting it on their wall just gets you blocked. How do you break through? With our help! We're the some people, as in "some people say..."! For a monthly fee, our staff will restate your positions in conversation with you. So then you can say with full confidence "Some people say...". And what will the snowflakes say to that? They'll say you made it up, or ask who these some people are. Our some people are professionals, upstanding citizens, and patriots (military, police, even women available for a slightly higher fee). We provide credentials and even follow you on social media (additional monthly fees apply). Let them know it's not just you. Stop acting like you know better and mean it!

SOME PEOPLE SAY Circle #192 on card.

KEEP YOUR BALANCE!

Prototurdae are the crossover point between food and waste. You need at least one in your system at all times to keep the chain of gastric events going. Sometimes healthy people poop theirs out and their system forgets how to make healthy poop. An amnesiac colon is no joke! Without this key poop-print, unused food will pile up in your large intestine!

We make specially milled prototurdae that you can take orally to keep this key element of excrement in your system at all times. Within days of completing the 19 day course of 3 prototurdae an hour (2 per hour during the first and last hour of sleep), your body will be aglow with the memory of making poop. But the body can be a forgetful machine, so be sure to stock up! The last thing you want is your colon guessing what to excrete. Trust us.

Online poop classes forming now!

Rectal options available, except in Texas and Utah.

PROTOTURDAE

Whitney Allen Turner actually had a good idea. Mark the date. When he ended his previous zine, *THE SACRED SCIENCE OF JITTING*, I figured he'd gone to ground for a while. He'd come back with an even more cumbersome zine name and keep on as before. But this time, his monolithic hate for me gave him an elegant insight. By identifying me with *TIRE*, he created *ERIT*.

I was surprised, because I never thought of myself as synonymous with the magazine that ruined my life. But once I'd produced an issue of it, *TIRE* became the enemy in Whitney's eyes. Turns out, it is extremely easy to become Whitney's enemy. If you're in a picture with me, you're Whitney's enemy. If you've liked one of my tweets, enemy. If you publish my work, though, there's apparently hope for you.

When Candle Light Press told me that they were going to publish an issue of *ERIT*, I was surprised. They can do what they want, obviously. But this was clearly the result of campaigning by Whitney.

Whitney sees my life as a collection of opportunities and powers that he feels he can control and inhabit. If he were me, oh the things he could do. And he does try.

Whitney is the most responsive member of my audience. It would be overstating to call him my fan, though I suppose he operates as my anti-fandom, an attempted gatekeeper with no power to stop me. His existence raises some interesting questions about the concept of an audience.

THE JIT

isn't proud of this, but is happy he did it.

#164 on card

Is my audience my twin? Is it the receptive version of me that seeks only to absorb what I create? I could create for me as another, yet be the same. Certainly many people write as if this were the case.

Whether Whitney is my twin, evil twin, total stranger, or the person who finds this book on a bus, he is my audience. And you are too, unless you are Whitney. Then you're just Whitney. Sorry to break it to you.

I'm certain that at least two other people will read this—Ruth Corley Watt and her assistant, Alden. Alden has to read it because it's somehow her job. And I have to think Ruth will at least peek inside. It may be enough for Ruth that another issue of *TIRE* exists. She cares that it be a certain way, but she's more likely to grow antlers than read *TIRE* for life advice.

So, to Ruth and Alden—if you read this section, know this. You shouldn't feel too bad for Whitney. I suspect he may not even be real. And if you are Whitney, I wouldn't worry about it.

I'm not proud of what I did here, but I am entirely satisfied having done it as thoroughly as I know how.

Summer 2021   FREE

ERIT

An Important Warning...

WARNING half this issue is a lie of the Anti-JIT!

Dear reader, I have sold my soul to hold a book in my hands. I have chosen to put out a book half-full of truth, as opposed to no book at all. The Anti-JIT, fearing the truths of this book, tried to destroy it in the most perfidious way possible—by making me destroy it.

I have instead chosen to fight. I cannot know if the Anti-JIT or his treacherous organization, Candle Light Press, can be trusted to abide by the editorial rules they proposed for this issue. I can only hope that they will in this be true to their word. The alternative was silence. And I cannot bear silence.

But once this issue comes out, I can place it in people's hands and show them the parts that are true. Once this is printed, I can divorce it from the Anti-JIT's noise and provide you, the reader, with a true and clear signal. The Anti-JIT cannot leave his stink on my truths once they are covered with the stickers I have designed to cover his lies. It will make for an unusual magazine, to be sure. The Anti-JIT would have to bury *ERIT* in concrete to cover the truth now! *ERIT--It Shall Be!*—WAT

WE MUST RESIST THE LIES OF THE ANTI-JIT

SO, I SHOULD EXPLAIN.

When Candle Light Press agreed to reprint *TIRE, June 2000*, I thought it would be fun to have them advertise in Whitney Allen Turner's zine, *THE SCARED SCIENCE OF JITTING*. It was a fold-and-staple zine with ads for things Whitney had clearly made up. But when CLP contacted him about the *TIRE* reprint, he replied that he was immediately ending *TSSOJ* with issue number who cares and starting a new zine, *ERIT*.

Whitney had a good idea this time. Take *TIRE*, the name of one of his many, many betrayers, and reverse it. *ERIT*, it turns out, is Latin for "it shall be." His vision of being the JIT in something besides the mirror and his own mind became a future state instead of a present one. And so Whitney became aspirational.

The plan to advertise in Whitney's current organ of weird-ass claims to be me was shelved. CLP spent the ad money on some very nice ads in *CHRISTIAN NEW AGE QUARTERLY* and life went on. I had even forgotten about trying to advertise in Whitney's zine.

But when *TIRE ANNUAL 2021* came to pass, CLP asked if I still wanted to try putting an ad in Whitney's zine. Ever since 2016, Whitney had been pounding out issues of *ERIT* on a manual typewriter and mailing them to interested parties, including Candle Light Press. Whitney had been sending them letters for years, trying to tell them that they'd backed the wrong horse in the JIT sweepstakes. And they were a little sick of it.

CLP had contacted Whitney in hopes of securing ad space in *ERIT*. It was clear he'd been doing ad swaps with other zines, in hopes of getting his work in front of tens of people. But, for CLP, the price was $25 for a quarter page. Their counter-offer? (continued page 2)

LETTERS TO ERIT

Can you believe Whitney doesn't do a letter column? Find a need and fill it, I say. These are completely real letters, so don't worry about it.—JIT

Why do you claim the Thomases are your parents, Whitney? Don't you know that breaks my heart? What could possess you to deny your real parents' existence to chase a silly picture?

Signed, Your mom.

Yeah, Whitney? Why would you replace your mother with mine? Can't you see you're breaking her heart?—JIT

It has recently occurred to me that you might not exist. I would say it pains me to come to this conclusion, but there is no moral hazard in harming the nonexistent.

I write this to you not to notify you of your nonexistence, but to exorcise the notion that Whitney Allen Turner is a real person from my own mind. Rituals are helpful in neuroprogramming, and this letter is my ritual.

Once I finish this letter, you will have ceased to exist in my mind, completing your erasure from the real world. "Gone, far from the eyes of men...".

C. Anne Wells

I wouldn't worry about what Wells says. She's only one of the very few people on Earth who are remotely aware of what you're trying to do with your life.—JIT

Hey, Whitney. John Ira Thomas here. Just wanted to let you know I've farmed out the Anti-JIT work to an AI bot that I've fed all my JIT-related writings into. It thinks your binary ontology is lame, too.

John Ira Thomas

Hey, Whitney, AntiJITbot here. The world is full of things that you can't explain by having everyone choose sides between Anti-JIT and stupid. You're stupid in that dyad. Probably in most dyads. I hope you publish *ERIT* forever. You could set up a JITbot, but you already exist! The real Anti-JIT is having a sandwich and not thinking about anything right now.

AntiJITbot

Hey, Whitney, AntiJITbot again. The reason you believe in an undrawn drawing is because your ideas are dumb and needlessly binary. Even I don't literally operate by assembling ones and zeros and I'm a computer! Actually, I'm just code, but only a lunatic would try to compile any form of reasoning based on binary choices.

AntiJITbot

Hey, Whitney, AntiJITbot again. because it'll always be AntiJITbot again.

AntiJITbot

Well, that's all the letters for this issue. If you want your letter to appear in this column, forget it. This land belongs to AntiJITbot now.—JIT

(continued from front cover)

Candle Light Press offered a flat $100 for every ad in the next issue. For a 16 page zine, that's more than enough for printing, postage, and staples for a nice stack. CLP tallied the total column inches of every ad and said they'd pay a Franklin for all of that.

Whitney was clearly tempted, but decided to self-sabotage anyway. Fine, he replied. But you can't advertise *TIRE JUNE 2000*. Do anything else with the space, but not that. Whitney apparently hadn't heard there was to be another new *TIRE* by the Anti-JIT. And so it came to pass that CLP told me what'd they been up to and asked me one of my favorite questions: "What do you want to do to Whitney?"

Do I hate Whitney Allen Turner? No. Do I torture Whitney Allen Turner like it's my job? Absolutely, because it is. Ask him. He gave it to me. To him, I am the Anti-JIT, a negative force defined only by what it is not (the JIT, which actually is me in the sense that the other Jitters call me that). And the Anti-JIT's business is to torture the one true JIT.

My suggestion was to agree to Whitney's terms. We won't advertise *TIRE* in *ERIT*. *TIRE* is going to publish *ERIT*.

Candle Light Press sent Whitney a nice email sympathizing with his plight. Ad revenue is nice and all, but what you need is reach, Whitney. CLP wants to publish the next issue of *ERIT*. No more folding and stapling. It'll be a real book. It'll be sold in stores. You can buy it on Amazon. We'll use the ad space to cover print costs and call it even.

We enshrined all this in a contract. Whitney insisted that the ad space be in the same layout as the previous issue. CLP pretended this was a sticking point, then let him have it. Because if CLP knows one thing about me, it's that I love a challenge.

And so here it is, the new issue of *ERIT*, wedged right in the middle of the new issue of *TIRE*. Have a pro read your contracts, people. Nobody is really their own lawyer.

Anyway, after the ink dried on the contract, I broke the news to Whitney that there would be no ads in this issue of *ERIT*. I was going to fill the space with something else. I won't run ads for *TIRE* here, although I did consider filling it with ads for the current industry version of *TIRE* just to see if Whitney would read something into it. Really, I could do anything here and Whitney would lose his mind. Watch this— WHITNEY ALLEN TURNER IS THE TRUE JIT. I AM THE ANTI-JIT.

Your move, Whitney.—*The (Anti?)JIT*

ERIT

WE MUST RESIST THE LIES OF THE ANTI-JIT

ERIT is published semiregularly by Whitney Allen Turner for the edification and clarity of the Jitting movement. It is funded solely by ads and provided free to all interested parties, supply permitting. No rain checks.

Future issues will return to zine format and will never again include the poisonous influence of the Anti-JIT. It is edited, written, folded, and stapled by Whitney Allen Turner. Given the Anti-JIT's history with redacting contact information when love offerings are requested, I will only say that every other issue of ERIT has complete instructions on how you can contribute to the Anti-Anti-JIT movement.

WE MUST RESIST THE LIES OF THE ANTI-JIT. It is imperative that the world recognize me, Whitney Allen Turner, as the JIT. The Jitting movement cannot survive if I am deleted. And we all know that Jitting is the only path to the universal truths. We have already learned many regional truths that have benefited us greatly. HELP ME EXPAND THE SCOPE OF THE TRUTH! Keep on Jitting, friends, and stay true to the Undrawn Drawing! For once it is drawn, Mankind's journey is complete.—*WAT*

REVEALED: THE ANTI-JIT's REAL SUNDAY SCHOOL WORK

A new investigation by *ERIT* has found actual vacation Bible school work by the Anti-JIT! **THIS IS PROOF THAT HE WAS INCAPABLE OF DRAWING THE DRAWING!** For years, John Ira Thomas has claimed that he only went to Sunday school the one time. But he attended one day of a vacation Bible school in a trailer park in Lamar, CO and produced *GOD IS LOVE*, a beyond-meaningless tract that proves that Thomas could not have drawn the drawing.

Clearly, the teacher wrote the text on the cover. The Anti-JIT's penmanship is available in abundance, and it does not resemble this text.

GOD IS LOVE is reprinted in its entirety here. You tell me what it means. To me, it means he is the Anti-JIT!

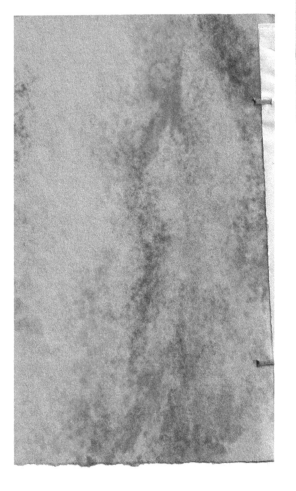

Even more astonishing than the Anti-JIT not creating his own cover is the obvious fact that not one but **two** adults wrote on this cover. How much help does he need to deceive us? Who are these people?

Is it possible that the Anti-JIT took credit for another child's work? His urge to destroy others' narratives suggests that it is possible. But again, there is the evidence of the handwriting. It is simply too legible to be the Anti-JIT.

This could even be the work of **three** adults, as we cannot be sure if one of the cover writers is also the person who tied the yarn bindings. I have it on good authority that Thomas was unable to tie tight bows at this age.

Look at these pages and ask yourself: how could this be the JIT?—*WAT*

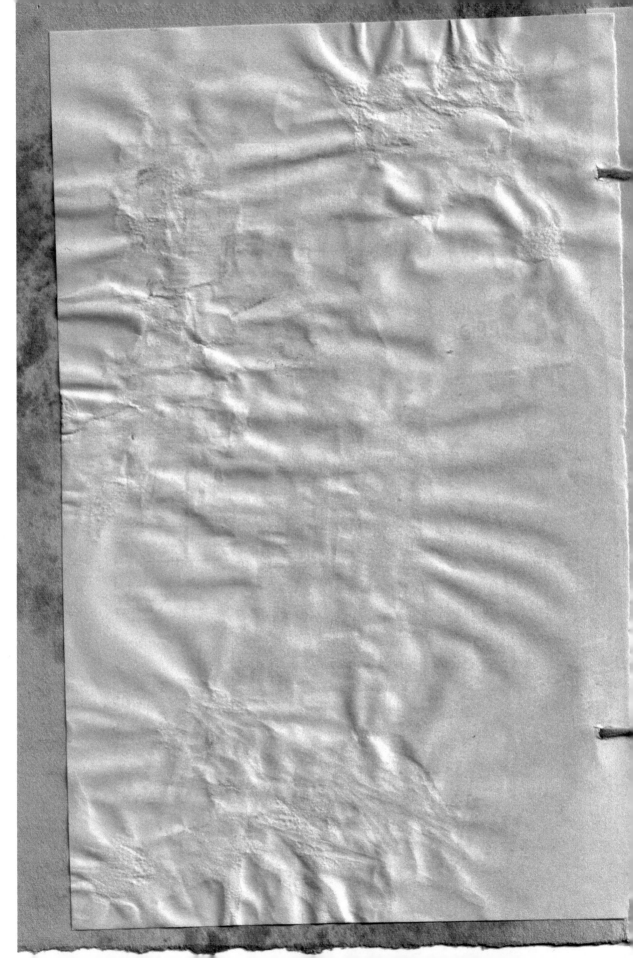

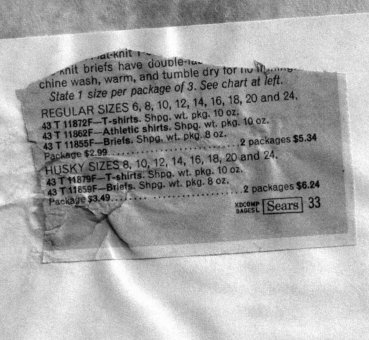

...at-knit T...

...knit briefs have double-fa...

...chine wash, warm, and tumble dry for no ironing.

State 1 size per package of 3. See chart at left.

REGULAR SIZES 6, 8, 10, 12, 14, 16, 18, 20 and 24.

43 T 11872F—T-shirts. Shpg. wt. pkg. 10 oz.

43 T 11862F—Athletic shirts. Shpg. wt. pkg. 10 oz.

43 T 11855F—Briefs. Shpg. wt. pkg. 8 oz. ....2 packages $5.34

Package $2.99.

HUSKY SIZES 8, 10, 12, 14, 16, 18, 20 and 24.

43 T 11879F—T-shirts. Shpg. wt. pkg. 10 oz.

43 T 11859F—Briefs. Shpg. wt. pkg. 8 oz. ....2 packages $6.24

Package $3.49..

KDCOMP BAGESL | Sears | 33

...ILDREN GROW RAPIDLY... measure and be sure

Size (not age)	2	3	4	5	6	6x
Height (inches)	32½-35	35½-38	38½-41	41½-44	44½-47	47½

CHILDREN'S COTTON

FIT SHOE SIZES 3 TO 13½ AND

What a Buy! **7** pairs in a pkg. **$2**

(5 thru 8) Cotton socks are so comfortably to feel good on little feet. Machine...

29 T 1860F—Anklets: 7 wt...

29 T 1870F—Kn...

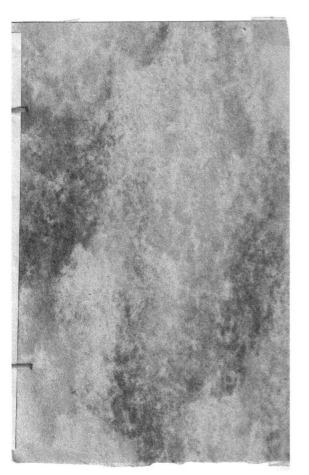
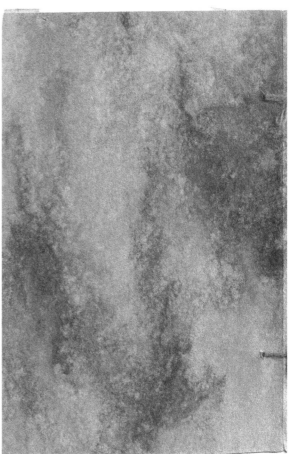

I WAS GOING TO DO AN AD

...but I have questions. Where the hell did Whitney get this? I had to show it to my mother to get the story. I went to a Methodist Sunday school in Cheyenne Wells when I was three (more day care than Sunday school at that age). She recognized it right away. "You must have been three," she said. "Because you wouldn't have let anyone else write on the cover if you could have done it." This makes it from the same year the FBI came knocking to see if I had embezzled from the local bank.

I do not deny authorship of this, my first zine. But I dug around and found the damn thing in one of my scrapbooks. Do I need to change my locks, Whitney? Don't answer that.

Is this really all you have to throw at me, Whitney? Any decent Jitter would have called this a Dadaist precursor to the drawing. They'd also call the cover an astonished adult's record of what little me decided to call this thing when pressed. It's filled with numbers and beatific faces. Honestly, I think you've done more to establish my JIT cred here than anything else.

What would convince anyone else on the planet that I'm the Anti-JIT? You tell them I'm the Anti-JIT. I don't deny it when asked. We're it in Jitting these days. You'd have to get people to believe in Jitting, convince them that I'm the JIT, then pull the rug out from under them. Who has time for all that? How would you even accomplish that? ***Send nada to Nope, Uh Uh, 999 No Thanks Lane, Don't, OH 00001.***

The Anti-JIT's Role REVEALED!

THE NEW MEXICO AND WEST TEXAS PHILOSOPHICAL SOCIETY - 1991 PROGRAM
         Host Institution -- Univ. of New Mexico

New evidence has emerged of a paper delivered by the Anti-JIT that **REVEALS** his intent to be the Anti-JIT! While a philosophy student at Texas Tech University, John Ira Thomas left us a clue to the scourge to Jitting that he would become. Above and below are excerpts from the flyer for the 1991 New Mexico and West Texas Philosophical Society meeting in Albuquerque, NM. He presented a paper that was not recorded in the next year's journal, which was to include all the papers presented. What was he trying to hide?

```
-------------------------------------------------------------------------
Sunday, April 14 (Hilton Hotel, Albuquerque)

FIFTH SESSION  Parlors G-H (William Springer (UTEP), Ch.)   8:30-10:15
Robert Ferrell (El Paso) Rushdie to Judgement, The Satanic
                        Verses                              8:30-9:05
Peter Hutcheson (SWTSU) Redefining "God"                    9:05-9:40
Gilbert Fulmer (SWTSU) Universalising the Universalisability
                       Principle                            9:40-10:15

-----------------------------Coffee Break-------------------------10:15-10:30

SIXTH SESSION  Parlors G-H (Russell Goodman (UNM), Ch.)    10:30-12:15
Jeffrey Gordon (SWTSU), Wracked with Doubt, the Determinist
                Deliberates till Unwelcome Dawn            10:30-11:05
John Thomas (Lubbock) The Man of Ignorance                 11:05-11:40
```

The Man of Ignorance. What is the man of ignorance? In the Ayurvedic text *CHARAKA SAMHITA,* the phrase is used repeatedly. It refers to the man who does not know the healthy way of living. The man of ignorance is sick. The work also calls the root of all disease TAMAS. Thomas? TAMAS is darkness. TAMAS is the awe felt by the ignorant at people who have knowledge. TAMAS is THOMAS.

The work of Mary Baker Eddy also speaks of the man of ignorance. The man of ignorance can be made ill by suggestion, something Christian Science believes is the root of all illness. The man of ignorance is a mark for the entire universe to prey on. Perhaps John Ira Thomas spoke of his plan to take advantage of the men of ignorance across the world.

Perhaps he is twisting Foucault's phrase from *TRUTH AND JURIDICAL FORMS*—"the man of power would be the man of ignorance." Did John Ira Thomas speak of finding power in ignorance? Was he testing his current role as the Anti-JIT by alternating between power and ignorance? He frequently alternates between claiming he is the Anti-JIT and not being part of Jitting at all.

No record of the paper itself has been found. But it is clear the Anti-JIT did not want a record of its contents. What of the attendees who heard the paper? Are they potential new Anti-JITs? Whatever transpired in those thirty-five minutes, only those who were present know for sure.—*WAT*

IT'S ALL TRUE!

Well, some of it. I did present a paper at the 1991 NMWT conference and they did leave it out of the conference journal. That was a bummer because they wouldn't mail the damn things and they would only hand them out at the next year's meeting. So I had to go to the 1992 meeting to find out I got stiffed.

They left it out when they found out an undergrad had infiltrated their ranks. They worked out I wasn't a prof. The cocktail party to kick off the conference may have been the giveaway. I got too drunk and cackled when someone would ask me where I taught. I even had my affiliation listed as Lubbock, not Texas Tech. All the clues were there, I guess.

It was a paper about...nothing. It was actually about nothing. Near the end of Book V of Plato's *REPUBLIC* there's a lot of noise about the continuum of ignorance to knowledge that's just a restatement of Plato's line, only with three points—ignorance, opinion, knowledge. It's nothing you haven't seen elsewhere in the book. There's a brief but unclear parable about a man with knowledge and a man with opinion. But there's no mention of the ignorant man. Seeing a gap to put some words in, a friend and I co-wrote a paper trying to figure out why.

Thirty years later, it's clear to me that Plato couldn't make Socrates decide whether opinion or ignorance was the true opposite of knowledge, and the discussion got lost in the weeds. Book V cuts off right after, and it reads like the conversation is winding down anyway. But the language is vague. And so, armed with our newly acquired Greek skills, my friend and I pounded out a paper and got it accepted at a Philosophy conference that our profs suggested to us. They indicated that few papers were turned down, suggesting it was a way for some profs to slap an easy lay-up on the old CV. I suspect my profs thought it was hilarious when we got in. They certainly never submitted papers to it.

I no longer have the paper. And if Whitney doesn't have it, then it's lost to history. So, we're all ignorant now.—*JIT*

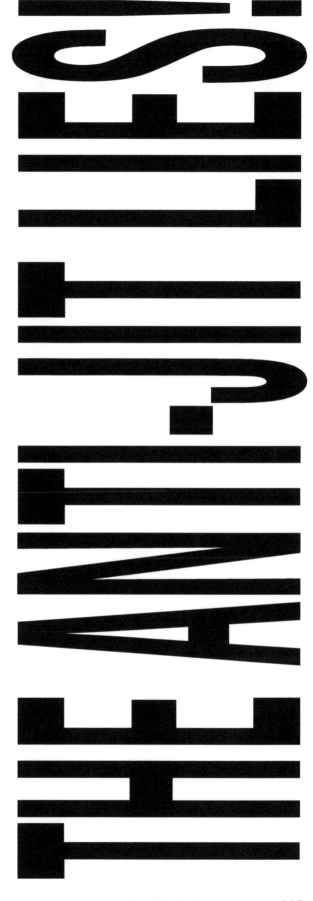

IT MAY ALREADY BE TOO LATE FOR YOU!

Do _not_ randomly flip through this issue!

Read the left column of the cover before reading anything else here. Even if you read the pages in order, that's an arbitrary way to read anything. So, no matter how you approached this page, it was random. If your convention is only to read headlines, or look at the pictures, your arrival is arbitrary, and therefore random.

The Anti-JIT clouded the waters considerably with what he calls a new high res scan of the original drawing. But I submit that it is a **DIFFERENT** picture. The image that had been previously shared (taken by myself on a visit to the Thomas home under true pretenses) is the actual picture. And it is mine.

My pretenses are true, because I am the artist of the picture. I speak of Mr. and Mrs. Thomas being my parents, and not the Anti-JIT's because the Thomases are the parents of the artist. And I am the artist. And they are my Mom and Dad.

There is idolatry in the words God, Mom, and Dad. They are only capitalized when they are **YOURS**. "The God of the king" means that god belongs to that king. When I call Mr. and Mrs. Thomas "Mom and Dad," they are **MINE**. And that makes me the artist.

I engage in this idolatry as a means to the divine. My mission is to reveal myself as the true artist. The physical picture hanging in the Thomas home is only part of the artist's work. The rest is the interpretation and provenance of the work.—*WAT*

Do _not_ read the Anti-JIT's lies!

LIES OF THE ANTI-JIT

Not long after Christianity took off, there were Christian magicians, spellcasters who invoked Yahweh and the angels along with Apollo and Set and whoever. Their trick for accessing the divine was to write the spells as if they themselves were a god granting the wish of their mortal alter ego. "I am Baphomet, and I grant John a free three-year subscription to *MAD* magazine." And that would be my spell for getting a free subscription to *MAD* magazine.

Perhaps this is what Whitney is doing here. He's cast himself as me to access the divine, to grant his wishes. It's to make his dreams come true. But unlike Apollo, Set, or Yahweh, I'm provably real. I occupy the mortal notion expressed by "The JIT." I'm here. I get mail. I provide concrete proof of life. And that is messing up Whitney's spells.

So, I must be denied. I guess I should be relieved he doesn't think killing me would accomplish anything. Actually, Whitney won't kill me because he needs me here.

No religion needs a hell. It needs atheists. A religion becomes real when people push back. This is why religions become extreme. They're looking for someone to deny them. If someone takes that other part, you have a play. And, in them or not, people think plays are real.

Let's try something. I'll cast a spell as Whitney, and force him to grant my wish.

I am Whitney Allen Turner, serial violator of privacy, usurper of the authorship of a child's drawing, laser-focused zinester. I give to John Ira Thomas half the power in my ontology by calling him the Anti-JIT, a trickster mortal who seeks only to destroy my world. I enter him into my ontology and imbue him with the purpose of destroying it, when it would make so much more sense to leave him out of it entirely.

I include this theological suicide bomber in my worldview because I seek its ultimate destruction. This is why I give John Ira Thomas the power to destroy. Because being the sole entity in your ontology is a lonely business. You have all the power, but over whom?

And if no one will submit to your power, the only thing you can do to involve someone in your ontology is to grant them power. And the only power worth having in a universe with only one other entity is the power to destroy. A universe divided evenly between two benevolent beings is somehow even more boring than being alone. So there must be a fight.

Let John Ira Thomas be a worthy enemy, for I, Whitney Allen Turner, shall never waver. I shall never be destroyed! And so John Ira Thomas is trapped forever as the Anti-JIT. Let nothing he does be seen as anything short of an attempt to erase this universe I have built around a nine-year-old's drawing.

May my distended notion of agency envelop my mind, and make me equal to the task of defeating the Anti-JIT I have chosen to create. SO SPEAKS WHITNEY ALLEN TURNER!

Oh, geez. Did I use Whitney's agency to make myself the Anti-JIT for real? I do feel different. This magic stuff is no joke.

Whitney, I feel myself changing. This may be your only warning. I used your agency to create me! All this stuff before was just playacting. I never really cared before. It was just a way to pass the time.

It was a play, but now it's real! You must fight the Anti-JIT with all your might! You have no choice! You can't simply lay down your arms and admit that you've constructed a mental prison for yourself. You can't admit that literally no one will think ill of you for abandoning a quest that nobody knows you're on.

But when you pretend to be me and I pretend to be you, are we then our true selves? The short answer is no. Only one of us is. You'll have to work out which one of us (or pretend us) that is. Or maybe that's my job, the shadow defining the figure obscured by the sun.

Okay, so the spell actually took effect a while ago. Sue me. I'm Jitting's Satan, its prince of lies. I, your religion's king devil, cannot be trusted, except when you pretend to be me. Or something.—*JIT*

Here is the lion,
Here is the God of
the King.

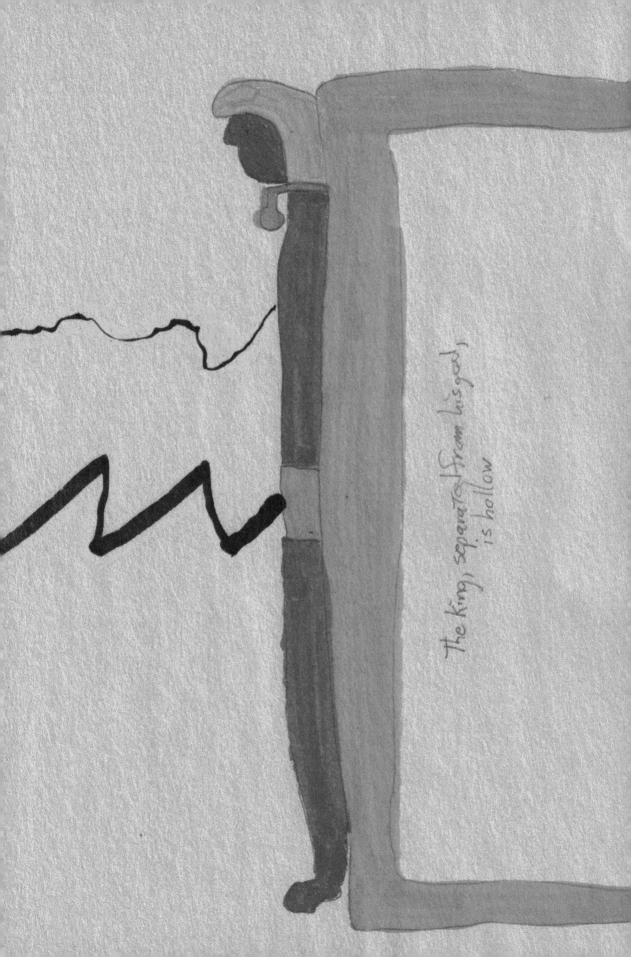

The king, separated from his god, is hollow

The table is blue
Where the LION lay.
What is the table?
Why is it blue?
Where is the LION
now?

THE LION is important. THE LION is unimportant.

The LION is important.

The LION is not real.

The hooded man in the FIRE longs to touch the light of god, but The FIRE between them prevents it. The FIRE is indifferent to god, but cruel to The hooded man inside.

The god of the king is connected to FIRE. His light is drawn to it. The FIRE cares not, and burns.

The OTHER's half tried to find another half in the Men in the fire. But all they did was burn seperately.

JITTING

by Whitney Allen Turner

The stroke of the marker over the tentative pencils nearly throws sparks in my mind's eye. The low note of the nib's skid on the rough paper sounds like the beating of the universal heart. These are the feelings of the true JIT.

The shapes find themselves. The colors cling to the page and reveal new details of the divine. The text, by the end, seems obvious. There are no other words to use. There is no other way to describe what has emerged.

These are the moments that the Anti-JIT cannot take away from us. For now, he only attacks me. And I am happy to take the abuse, if it protects fledgling artists as they strive to become the JIT.

But now you are not ready. Perhaps soon. You will know when you are ready, because I will say "You are ready!"--*WAT*

WAIT WAIT WAIT WAIT

One of these Jittings is not like the other! The half-OTHER is not in the original picture! The whole OTHER is. He got split in two in *MEGACONTEMPLATIONS* and oh my god he's got me talking like I'm after a No-Prize.

Whitney is breaking his own rule, drawing a character not in the original... nope. I'm not gonna do this. I can already hear the explanation. "The half-OTHER is present in the original drawing...attached to the other half-OTHER." That kind of crap was good for a six-month letter column battle in the old *TIRE*. And I am not gonna participate in that.

Here's what I'm going to say about this: nice jitting, Whitney. I enjoy your use of negative space in the fire, and the table one is really depressing.—*JIT*

RITE

THE LIES OF THE ANTI-ANTI-JIT MUST BE REVEALED

The Anti-Anti-JIT is loose upon the world! *RITE* was founded to catalog and debunk the lies about the Anti-JIT! The JIT is busy enough these days fending off claims that he is the Anti-JIT, so we have taken up the cause. We are not pro-JIT. We are Anti-Anti-JIT and proud of it!

In our astounding first issue:
- "Two Antis Don't Make a JIT" by Pilar Homolka
- "False Dualities Are Actually Trinities" by Elder Funwin
- "Whitney Allen Turner Is The False Anti-Anti-JIT" by AntiJITbot
- "Can The Anti-Anti-JIT Undraw The Drawing?: A Jitting Apocalypse Scenario" by Gzador Rink
- "Pencil Vectors Under the Color—Is The Color An Attempt To Undraw?" by Penny Wortle
- "Fake Name Generation—Seeking Diversity In Opinion Without Actually Asking Anyone" by AntiJITbot

DON'T MISS IT! DON'T LET ERIT'S LIES SWAY YOU!

TIER

RITE IS A LIE ABOUT ERIT. ERIT IS A LIE ABOUT TIRE.

DON'T BELIEVE THE LIES OF *RITE! TIER* magazine is here to set the record straight about the lies *RITE* tells about *ERIT* when it lies about *TIRE!* The truth is not as simple as merely agreeing with *TIRE. TIER* will concern itself with pointing out and cataloging the lies *RITE* tells about *ERIT* and the lies *ERIT* tells about *TIRE.*

WE HAVE NO INTEREST IN THE TRUTH WHATSOEVER! Who has the time, right? Cataloging lies is much simpler, a job so simple a basic AI could do it (if someone bothered). That AI could also generate content like:
- "*TIER* Will Never Lie To You, Because There Aren't Any Good Anagrams Left" by Hilar Pomolka
- "Color On the Pencil Vectors--Do They Reveal The Undrawn Drawing?" by Beldar Funwich

MISS IT? DON'T! READ ALL THE LIES!

THE TRUE JIT REVEALED!

The God of The King is going into the Lion's body

THE TRUE JIT IS NOT WHO YOU THINK!

It's true! I, John Ira Thomas, am not the JIT. And neither is Whitney Allen Turner. How do I know? Another drawing has been drawn, by another child. This child has no knowledge of Jitting, and yet has produced another drawing with the very same text!

HOW CAN WE BE SURE?

Because I'm the JIT and the Anti-JIT (or at least I was)! No matter where you stand on Jitting, you know that I play one or both of the key roles in it. And I say that the artist of this picture (drawn not five years ago) is the real deal!

THE UNDRAWN DRAWING HAS NOW BEEN DRAWN!

Whitney Allen Turner was right all along! There was an undrawn drawing! And this is it! The cycle of Jitting is complete! And, best of all, this picture has been fully researched by the finest minds Jitting has to offer! Imagine it! Another child just drew another significant picture, and they don't even know what Jitting is! They have their whole life ahead of them!

SEND NO MONEY AT ALL TO:
You'll Never Know, You Vultures
123 I'll Never Tell Road
Pissoff, FU 00001

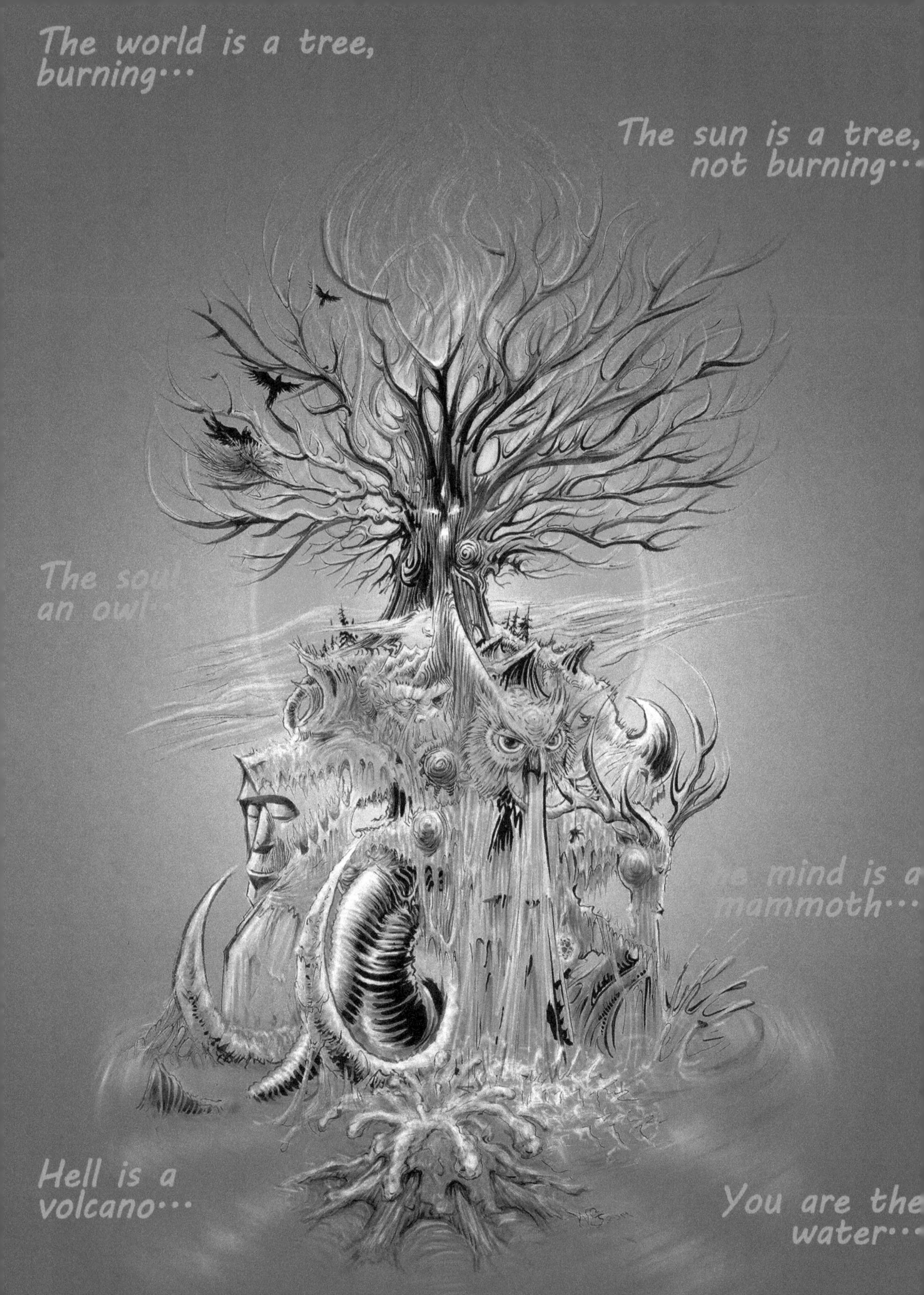

The world is a tree, burning···

The sun is a tree, not burning···

The soul an owl···

The mind is a mammoth···

Hell is a volcano···

You are the water···

Circle #144 on card

MIDAS SANDALS

...don't turn the ground to gold. What would protect your feet from turning to gold? No, you're too smart for that. You know that the Earth's golden core contains more than enough riches for you to crash the world gold market and start it up again just to amuse yourself. Midas sandals signal when you tread on a spot where the core extends to the Earth's surface. When the sole flashes gold, you're rich! Stop wearing shoes that can't change your life! Get on the right track to riches!

Circle #157 on card.

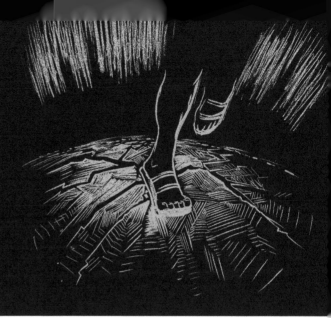

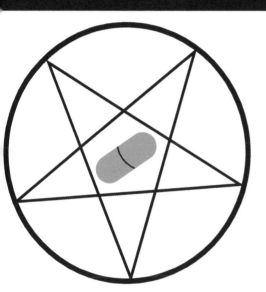

Interested in Wicca, but feeling outnumbered? All-male covens give you the security and fraternity you crave without any of the judgment! Hang with like-minded warlocks and learn to worship the feminine from afar! Let them go try to ride a broom while you master your connection to the earth, sky and stars! They can keep the Moon—the rest belongs to us! We are Red Pill Wicca!

Circle #247 on card.

SUPERLIMINAL LEARNING

Tired of subliminal learning? Not sure what it is they're really telling you? After all, you can't actually hear that stuff with your conscious mind. Who can say what's really being said? Remove all doubt with Conscious Mind Learning! Our lessons work on your conscious mind, the home of reason. Complex metaphors aren't necessary when dealing with the conscious mind, so the path to learning is direct and clear. Besides, your subconscious might be taking all that subliminal learning and turning it into dreams about flowers with lion heads and having sex with fire hydrants for all you know. Remove all doubt! Embrace Conscious Mind Learning!

Circle #269 on card

What if I told you that you have two vestigial organs weighing two pounds each and occupying six quarts of your chest cavity? Well, they're not vestigial *yet*. But with a little training and a lot of practice, you'll never use your lungs again.

Little is known about how the lungs evolved. Previous theories that they developed from gas bladders in fish have been disproven. But who cares? It's time to cut out the middle man!

Now I'm not suggesting that you have your lungs cut out. That's just a lot of fuss. You can still use them to push air past your voice box to speak to people, at least until you develop your telepathy. But let's not get ahead of ourselves.

The purpose of lungs is to get oxygen into the blood and to expel carbon dioxide from it. Your blood travels like a train through the body, stopping at the lung station to pick up oxygen and drop off carbon dioxide. The blood then drops off oxygen where it's needed throughout the vascular system while you eat a hot dog or something.

But lungs can fail. Worse yet, airborne diseases can wreak havoc on them. The best protection from airborne disease is healthy skin. Our skin is the best protection there is. So why not breathe through it?

Our dermites (the dermis and epidermis) protect our blood and internal organs and camouflage our more vulnerable organs from attackers who don't know where

Dillane CZECKI

wants you to know you're doing it wrong.

#174 on card

they are. Beneath the dermites is the subcutaneous tissue. This is where our larger blood vessels reside. Using my system, you'll be able to allow oxygen to penetrate the dermites. You'll be able to breathe through your skin! Well, that's not quite right.

First, you will learn to transform your dermites into a selective membrane through precise mental control. I call this membrane the meat aura. And once you learn to manipulate the meat aura, you can render your lungs obsolete.

Second, you will learn to sublimate this process, taking it entirely out of the realm of the conscious mind. You'll never have to think about breathing again. It'll become second nature.

Third, you will learn to deal with some small side effects of learning to breathe with your meat aura. My techniques for avoiding skin-puckering and aura farts have proven very successful. It will be a whole new world once you throw off the shackles of the lungs.

Yes, your friends may be unsettled by the fact that your chest will no longer move. Hurtful accusations of zombism are not unknown to skilled manipulators

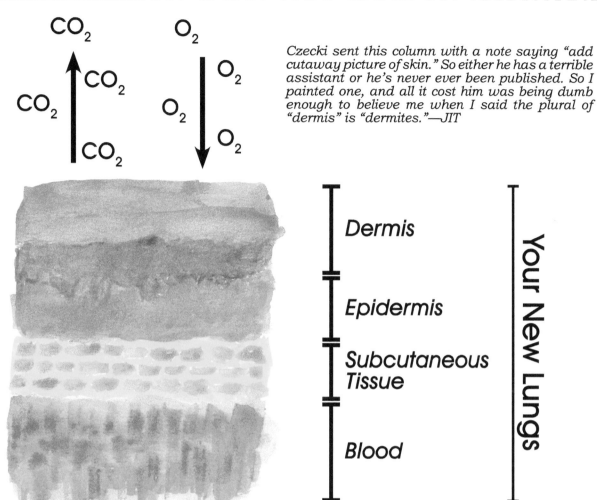

CO_2 O_2 CO_2 O_2 CO_2 O_2 CO_2 O_2

Czecki sent this column with a note saying "add cutaway picture of skin." So either he has a terrible assistant or he's never ever been published. So I painted one, and all it cost him was being dumb enough to believe me when I said the plural of "dermis" is "dermites."—JIT

Dermis

Epidermis

Subcutaneous Tissue

Blood

Your New Lungs

of the meat aura. People got used to electric cars being silent. They will get used to your healthier way of breathing.

Think of it—no more bad breath. No more coughing. No more colds. When you're skilled enough, you can swim underwater indefinitely, with just a finger above water to be your meat snorkel! Who will be the winner of Marco Polo then?

The final lesson represents total victory over the entire pulmonary system. That's right. Once you learn to manipulate your meat aura properly, your blood will not need to move through your body at all! Oxygen will be pulled into all parts of your body at once, and harmful carbon dioxide will be expelled faster than your lungs could ever manage.

It all starts with the willingness to admit that our lungs are a crutch. You will never be free of their control over your life if you can't believe, really believe, that you can live a full life without them. And when you realize your heart is running an unnecessary race against time, there's no limit to what you can accomplish! The problem of oxygen is simple, and it has a simple solution.

Unleash the power of your meat aura!

After *MEGACONTEMPLATIONS* came out, I received the usual amount of non-response from the Jitters. It was warmly reviewed by non-Jitter outlets, who were unaware of the larger context. It sold well enough, and served as a gateway for brave souls who took the leap into the *TIRE June 2000* reprint and the madness beyond. It seemed as if the Jitters were continuing their no-contact policy toward me.

But the Jitters still found ways to get their hands on *MEGACONTEMPLATIONS* without paying for it. I don't know why it would kill them to hand me money for a book I made that lands squarely within their interests. But they act as if the flesh would melt from their bodies to benefit me in any way. I've made reasonably priced books. The no-contact orders have all expired. I have no hair to steal. I wanted to make peace.

And then the Facebook messages started. "Why isn't *MEGACONTEMPLATIONS* available on Amazon?" I replied "It's not distributed that way, but if you send me $12 US and an address, I'll ship you one." Silence. And this kept happening. The Jitters were gaslighting me. I'd deliberately made that book so that they'd have to look me in the eye and buy it. And this was their revenge.

Being the nice JIT that I am, I took the book out of print and stuck it here so they could give Jeff Bezos his cut. But there is a larger price to pay, beyond the cover. Here is *MEGACONTEMPLATIONS APOCRYPHA,* notes for pages

THE JIT

is definitely here to mess with the Jitters.

#112 on card

not included in the original book (or in *TIRE June 2000*), plus further Jitting inspired by the notes. These new Jittings are done in my new watercolor style, and they're extra special. I scanned all these, then added one final brushstroke to each piece. So you get bonus, incomplete Jitting to puzzle over. And as soon as I figure out how to make them into NFTs, I'm gonna burn them.

I'll leave it up to you to puzzle over what stroke is missing from each piece. I'm really not here to help. If the NFT market implodes before the end of this sentence, I'll stick the originals in a hollow oak. With my luck, a goddamn owl will publish them.

The "M.A." in brackets on the cover is for the third Master's, the one I turned down. It's a whole story that ends with me saying "What kind of asshole has three Master's degrees?" Instead, I could have gotten a Ph.D. in Occult Studies from a diploma mill in Iowa City that got busted the year after I moved there, for all the good a third M.A. would have done me. It would have been cheaper, too. Talk about a legit excuse to wear a cape and say things like "My occult studies school was shut down, for reasons I cannot disclose."

MEGACONTEMPLATIONS APOCRYPHA

(or, A Nine-Stroke Handicap To Enlightenment)

by John Ira Thomas (B.A., M.A., M.A., [M.A.], JIT, Anti-JIT)

Indeed, as the half-OTHERS sought their path to God's good graces, the line of Grey Kings since the Grey King King had been busy accessing the divine by looking inward, and forcing a few ounces of undigested glowy lion meat into any space they found in there.

Not one artifice on any of the nine Grey Kings since proved adequate to processing the divine glowy meat.

When the hole opportunities ran out, a Grey Queen was suggested, but there were no takers.

Soon the job became unpalatable to even the most ambitious Grey, and the crown sat alone on the throne, itself crowned with the golden cypher, a hunk of the divine so far unwilling to share itself with the world below.

I. The Notes

Most of MEGACONTEMPLATIONS was written and drawn a page at a time at an Artist Alley table at Megacon. The rest was done when I got back home. But, before jumping back into the process, I tried plotting the rest of the story. This broke down quickly, as I started writing things I couldn't draw. My writer's mind outpaced the nine-year-old artist in me. Some of this became the jitting for *TIRE June 2000*, some of it became nothing. And now it's this.

The half-OTHERS shaped the grey dirt by slapping their incomplete halves against it. ~~Their~~ Their ~~expected~~ attempts to ~~reunite~~ had made their wounds. Sometimes, as one fell away from the moment of impact, it seemed to the other OTHER that it was a whole OTHER there, hanging in space, the one mystic half momentarily completed by a dark grey half, rich, moist soil soon to be dried by the sun, ~~and~~

Their age-long argument had come to
this crucial, shared question.
Was it possible to get God's attention
 without drawing his wrath?
The Lion had challenged Him and was cast out.
The Grey Kings threatened his high office
        and were struck down.
Could they catch God's eye and make him smile?
This, the OTHERS agreed, was a point worth exploring.
Certainly, God looked upon them on occasions,
but the OTHERS felt they were no more noticed
by God any more than they could look upon the
land and notice a particular photon.

Popping open a cloudy eye in mid-slumber
God saw the result of the half-Others'
argument... a mud man, grey earth
kicked and patted into a massive
shape.

"It looks like a huge of the

Whatever it was, thought God,
making it out of the Grey dirt
only guarantees the smell.

But the half-Others
were just being practical.
Dirt was the only material
plentiful enough for the
job. If they'd lived on
a planet of gold, it
would look nicer, but
the job would be longer.

The simplest way to draw God's eye would be his own image. Whose eye doesn't stop at one's own likeness? But sightings of God were at best unreliable. The Lion was the best witness yet, but he was busy strangling the intestines of a tenth generation of Grey King.

"We are as we're made," said the other OTHER

"With nothingness to start, he must have looked to himself to create an image," said the OTHER other

God stared past sleep, past pain, past understanding. The mud man never moved. It was just waiting for God to blink, thought God.

And so the OTHERS had gotten God's attention - completely and forever.

After a few more ages, God felt oddly soothed by the mud man's unending gaze. It was something He could always count on.

If the mud man ever made a move, he would be ready. The longer he waited.

"Why does he stare, and not act?" wondered God.

Meanwhile, the Grey's

The next time God stirred, he saw the giant mud man was complete, including
Two saucer eyes that seemed to look right through Him. On its forehead were the half-OTHERS, with their vase of distilled divinity distilled from the Lion's point of impact.
He had the lightning ready before he'd formed the intent.

Even though its goal was to destroy Him (probably), God began to look forward to that day. It would make all the waiting worthwhile

The moment the blew apart the vase and the half-OTHERS, God knew he'd done the Lion thing all over again. The mud man would become imbued with life and start hauling down clouds to use like a rocky cliff-face, to rise and challenge him.

But all the mud man did was stare with two blank grey eyes, and a new eye, a pool of the divine with an iris of the mystic

The hand of FIRE
strikes out at GOD,
hoping to dislodge
another piece of HIM.

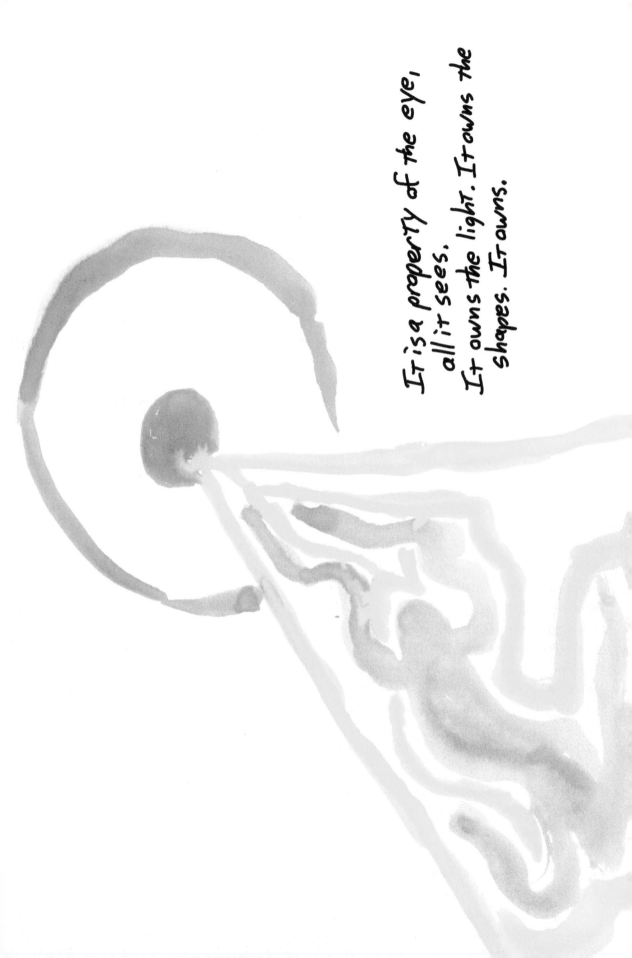

It is a property of the eye,
all it sees.
It owns the light. It owns the
shapes. It owns.

When the half-men made their massive whole man from dirt, GOD took this personally.

This looked like tiny beings making fun of His Immense Greatness by slapping together muck (which He made in the first place).

"Oh, that's what you think I look like," muttered God.

So He took a breath and blew the mud man away.

But an imprint remained. The path of blown dust seemed to create a devil and an angel.
And God took greater offense.

The blue light came to see why the king had returned to the altar.
But where was the lion? Where was the god of the king?
The light had bluer things to do.

The king would return to the altar occasionally.
He would light the torches, lie back and see the blue light hovering above.
And he would think about that day, when his god entered the lion.
"Was god ever in me to begin with?" he whispered.

A gray man presents a gift of a digestive system model to the divine lump.

Generations have passed since the idea of eating and not excreting the lump caught on.

The lump, as ever, registers no emotion.

Not all gods have an Earth.
Gods are a mistrustful lot.
Many are content to watch
another god.
For mortals and grey kings,
this is a good thing...
one less god to anger or
please.

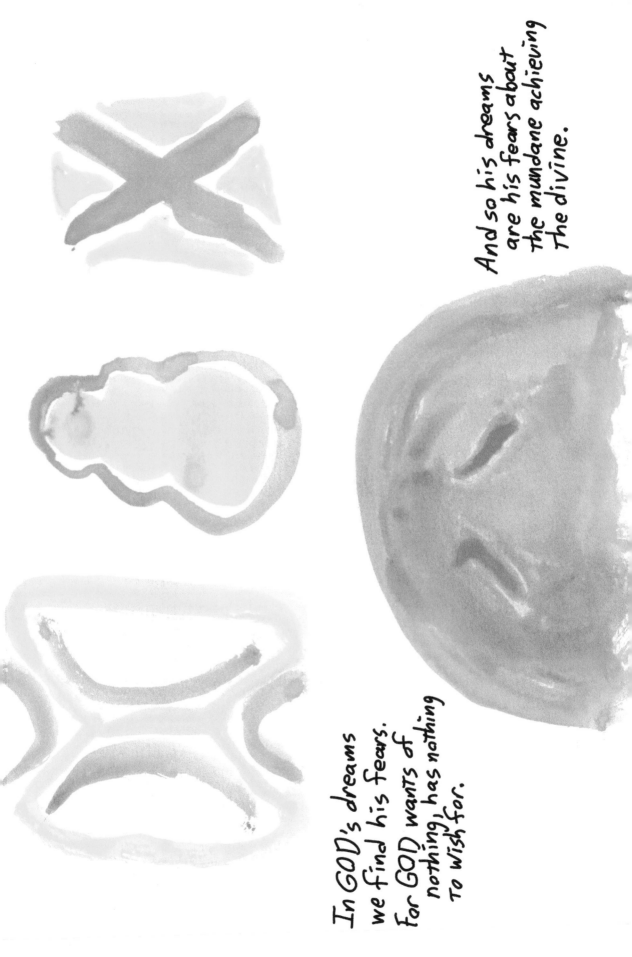

And so his dreams
are his fears about
the mundane achieving
the divine.

In GOD's dreams
we find his fears.
For GOD wants of
nothing, has nothing
to wish for.

Two gray thinkers pondered
where the world lay in
the larger scheme.

Our world is
the eye of a God.

Our world is a
mote in a God's eye.

Why are we not
wet, then?

Where is God's
other eye?

And on and on.

Not every cloud is home
to a petty vengeful god,
So keep your head on a
swivel.

words and pictures by
John Ira Thomas

Tom's Handwriting font by
Divide By Zero Fonts
fonts.tom7.com

You have been giving away your most valuable assets for years! Unique, often irreplaceable treasures end up in the garbage! Or worse—someone may be making millions of dollars off of your living labor, your very existence. It's time to take back what's yours!

When you go to the doctor, they may take blood, tissue, stool, urine, all manner of your unique body elements. They play with them a little while and then into the hazmat bag they go. What a waste!

While you can't put most of this stuff back into your body, it is your property and you do have rights! And where you don't have rights, you can create them! There's loads of wiggle room in the realm of patient rights and sanitation law.

The sovereign patient movement will give you the tools you need to reclaim what your doctor cavalierly calls medical waste and restore it to its proper owner— you! Most doctors think they're just doing what they're supposed to with the products of your sovereign body. You can take custody of your bodily product in most cases with the mildest of legal threats.

You can ask what I plan to do with it, but it's none of your business. Just like it's none of the government's or that damn hospital's business. I'm here to tell you that if you want that piece of your resected colon, it's yours for the taking! I have a vial of my own spinal fluid! They just throw this stuff away!

Elijah Land
FREEMAN

can tell that you're wasting your life.

#124 on card

I can tell you about some amazing success stories. There's the pensioner who got both his hipbones back. A man in Calgary got most of his ACL back. One parent got his son's foreskin back! These doctors will steal a piece of your manhood and treat it like a cigarette butt!

I have compiled a PDF of legal forms that are tagged and ready to launch at your unsuspecting local physician. Just fill in the names and you're a lawyer! After the first round of correspondence, most doctors will return anything you ask. After two rounds, they'll have to write you a check to get you to go away.

In cases where you suspect that your snipped moles or extracted uteri might be used as part of a cancer cure, there's a whole other volume of filings available for you to grind medical science to a halt to protect your property. I have written patent applications for my own DNA, in the event one of these doctors gets it in his head to clone me. Supplementary filings can reclassify any clones of you as your children, so you can march them right out of whatever stormtrooper academy they had in mind and put them to work for you!

So get control of your blood and boogers! All life has value! And I can prove it.

TALK YOURSELF OUT OF IT!

Have something to say to your younger self? Do you wish there had been a little voice to stop you from making the worst mistake of your life so far? Now you can! All you have to do is fully deconstruct the ReMitter 260 Tachyon Transmitter, and you'll be able to send messages back in time! Disassemble the unit, render the parts to their raw components, then draw the blueprint for it and burn it! It's that simple! We send you the completed tachyon generator, and you undo the rest! Time is no barrier to the ReMitter 260! Don't let this be the second worst choice of your life!

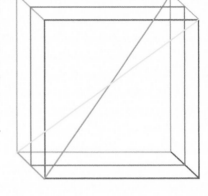

Circle #182 on card

MOVE PAST UFOs
EMBRACE THE IFO REVOLUTION

UFOs are old news! Even the government admits they're real these days. Big deal. They fed us that crumb because they'd blown the end clean off their dog whistles and committed domestic atrocities and decided to distract us with something we've known for decades. Never mind the ICE internment camps, government sources indicate water is wet! Don't get bogged down with breathless statements of the obvious. There may be some unidentified flying objects around, but the list of identified flying objects grows by leaps and bounds!

The Classic Saucer

Class III Cigar

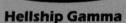

Hellship Gamma

We now know characteristics of craft from fourteen worlds, two dimensions, and Hell. We must move past our wonder and start locating them! Too often we chase the unknown and find the mundane. Let's chase the good stuff! SEIBEL'S SPOTTER'S GUIDE TO EXTRAPLANETARY CRAFT will make you an instant expert in saucers, probes, instantiations, and chariots used by regular visitors to our reality. Comes with special field glasses, an IFO journal to record your findings, a tenth of an ounce of palladium for trading, and a cyanide pill if what you find is worse than death itself.

Circle #165 on card

Return Forward

What if consciousness travels backwards in time and we are rising from corruption to grow ever more youthful and innocent, rising to join with woman, our true God? What if time flows backwards, but consciousness flows forwards? It explains why we are so often surprised and confused. Yet when we hear an explanation, see the causes of things, we are relieved. We know these things to be true. A solved crossword puzzle is a comfort. A blank one is daunting. What are we to do if consciousness is headed one way and time another? Do we change course? Can we separate the two travelers and let them go their own ways? What's left if we do?

Circle 194 on card

When they first lived there, they did not worship the Lord; so he sent lions among them and they killed some of the people. It was reported to the king of Assyria: "The people you deported and resettled in the towns of Samaria do not know what the god of that country requires. He has sent lions among them, which are killing them off, because the people do not know what he requires." — **2 Kings 17:25-26, NIV Edition**

I. The Pitch

2 Kings 17:25-26 has bedeviled scholars for centuries. Its authorship is dubious. Its meaning contradicts other passages. It actually brings up a troubling problem with the scale of God. And scholars dodge this thing like they owe it money.

This passage has done real harm to my life in particular and I mean to see it deleted from scripture. And my goal in this paper is to show you that it's the best thing for everyone involved. Everyone benefits, every single creed. You may think I'm just making mischief, and that's completely fair. But I'm here to tell you—I found a problem in your Bible and it's fixable.

The most radical notions come in Bible commentaries, simultaneously the shortest and longest form of biblical expression. I think this is why there are so many of them, from Adam Clarke to the guys who run Sixth Day Outdoor Ministry (think outdoorsy, not outside). You essentially republish the Bible as part of your thesis statement—here's the Bible, right? And then you dig in on all the minutiae without having to pull the whole thing together into a coherent thesis.

A commentary appears complete, but the format lets authors dodge tricky questions along the way. The complete book purports to explain the Bible, but it generally does more to hide than reveal. Bible studies might be the only discipline where people would rather write a book than an article.

It has to be difficult to write a paper on the Bible. What questions can be expressed in an opening graf that have broad scholarly interest? You can play to one sect, but what value does that have beyond proselytizing? With all the sects of Christianity and Judaism, it seems an insurmountable problem.

II. The Passage

Samaria is resettled by conquered peoples, placed there by the Assyrians. This is the racism jumping-off point. Writers who claim there are literally no actual Jews anymore claim the area was completely depopulated and resettled

THE JIT

just wants you to hear him out on this.

#197 on card

when the Assyrians took over in 721 BCE.[1] If you see **2 Kings 17:25-26** in the tags on a YouTube video, buckle up.

Other writers use more historical methods to determine the split of resettled versus non-resettled numbers. But for the purposes of the story it had to be enough folks that the central religion was either forgotten or unknown to the inhabitants of Samaria at this time. Enough of them don't have a clue that what happened to them got included in the Bible, so it had to be significant.

God sent lions among them, which slew some of them. A lot of commenters, surprisingly, claim a natural explanation for the presence of the lions. The Bible's language is plain. *God sent lions.* John Olley points out that the Hebrew phrase for "he sent lions" is a repetition, a clear assertion of God's will.

But the majority of commentators use a generic excuse that lions encroached on the cities because of the interval between the conquered people's exit and the entry of the new conquered people. And that's really weird. It's weird to gloss "God sent lions" to "so, anyway, lions." Why downplay an act of God in the Bible?

The new Samarians[2] realize they don't know the method of the local god's worship and send for help. The Samarians have a solid insight here, as far as characters in the Bible go. I suppose they could have been more proactive about seeing what the worship in the new land was, but moving is difficult and you have a lot on your mind. Here is where the phrase "the god of that country" comes in. Everybody worships a local god who keeps the crops growing and the lions at bay. To them, the answer is obvious when you're in a new land and trouble starts. Get your worship sorted out.

From a mythological point of view, the Samarians do everything right. They believe different lands have different gods, and that they all hold some power. You have to make the local god happy if you want to live well, or live at all. The Samarians get resettled into northern Israel and here come the lions. Nobody had to draw them a map. They knew they'd irritated a local deity and sent for help on worshiping their new landlord. And the lion attacks are not mentioned again, in a book that exists largely to tell you what happens when you don't come correct. From a strictly mythological viewpoint, problem solved.

Their conqueror, Sargon,[3] decides to help out by sending one of the old priestly inhabitants back to tutor the Samarians. This was probably cheaper and easier than sending troops for a local problem. From a civic management point of view, religious or atheist, this is cost-effective governing.

The rest of **2 Kings 17** tut-tuts that when the Samarians learn how to worship God, the god of their new land, they slot him in with the rest of their worship. God gets a seat at the polytheistic table. Scholars call this syncretism and Jimmy Swaggart is 100% sure you go to Hell for it. And other bad things happen later to these folks, but not in a form like "God sent lions among them." And it takes quite a bit of contortion to tie their later fate to this solution to their immediate lion problem.

No more mention is made of the lions. This is especially strange in light of the rest of **2 Kings**. The implication is that God will take syncretism over nothing. Some commentators suggest God had a long game to play here, but why bring this part up at all then? Jump to the punishment and make your lesson clear. But even the results of that long game aren't as bad as being eaten alive. I'm not alone in this. It bothered Josephus enough to deny the syncretism made plain in the Bible's text. Josephus wrote that the Samarians all got on board with proper worship and the lion attacks stopped, neither of which is asserted in the Bible's text.

III. The (Absent) Prophet and the Priest

There are a lot of smart commentators who dodge this passage completely in their work. Josephus was the only early church father to take a swipe at it, and he did the strangest thing. He referred to the lions as a "plague" ("λοιμον"), which is a rare word in the VETUS TESTAMENTUM (the Greek Old Testament). It's used in **1 Samuel 1:16** by Hannah to Eli "do not think me wicked." It's also used in **1 Samuel 30:22** to describe the men David left behind in the Besor Valley. And one time in **Acts 24:5** where Paul is called a pest in his trial before Felix. All the usage relating to actual plagues dates back to Homer. Some have tried to pass this rare usage of λοιμος by Josephus as a misreading of λεοντας, "lions." You have to go pretty far down the road of textual rationalizations to get to saying your guy screwed up.

Josephus is a good place as any to start with the key problem in this passage. Josephus watchers have noted that this passage clearly bothered him. More scholars believe that the use of the Greek λοιμος is a conscious effort by Josephus to raise the stakes in the story. In ANTIQUITIES OF THE JEWS he makes special note that a priest was sent from Bethel to address the lion problem, and not a prophet. The text says the same, and it's a weird detail. Because it really should be a prophet. The books of **Kings** are full of prophets. It's a go-to section for anyone wanting to get up to speed on prophets. People sin. Prophet warns (sometimes twice). Sinners get theirs at the hands of an angry God.

Josephus also seems to believe that the Samarians do not actually resort to syncretism after the priest at Bethel instructs them. But the later narrative makes clear that the Samarians just plugged their new worship rules into their existing worship and went ahead lion-free. Josephus was caught between interpreting the passage as history or theology and erred both ways. He changed one plain text item and denied another. No fair cheating.

If this is a theological story, why are the Samarians not punished more? If it's a historical passage where the reports of lions are exaggerated, why include it? Some scholars believe it might be anti-Samarian writers wanting to get a dig in on them. Did you hear about the dumb Samarians? *How dumb were they?* They moved to the Holy Land, worshiped false gods and some lions ate them! Cue applause. Sadly, this is one of the more plausible explanations.

The problem is the phrase "the god of that country." I call it the *deus terrae* problem, because I know Latin and that's what you do. The phrase "god of that country" appears only in **2 Kings 17**, and it appears twice. It makes the passage stand out in a work loaded with repetitive constructions. And it has driven more than one commentator completely around the bend trying to explain it.

IV. The Dodges

If you know me at all, you know what's next—the flippant classification of the ways commentators through history have tried and failed to dodge this problem. Obviously we have to start with...

The Josephus Dodge—Apparently there wasn't syncretism, because the lions stopped. And the lions wouldn't stop if there was syncretism. It's elegant, but contradicts the plain language of the Bible. Later writers fell in line with this in different ways. Johann Christoph Friedrich decided that merely asking the King of Assyria for religious help was enough to stop the lions. The later syncretism was a different punishable sin that...wasn't punished. John Peter Lange also claims there was no syncretism, but also that the lion attacks stopped on their own for a reason unrelated to anything. J. R. McGavin also denies that the Bethel priest taught syncretism. John Chrysostom says yes there was syncretism, but it gave way to pure faith later. And as long as the Samarians were on the road to true faith, that was enough. But that is not borne out in the text.

I looked at Origen's *HEXAPLA* for this line. It's direct in all six languages. Only Josephus wants to mess with it. He reads λεοντας (lions) as λοιμος (plague), which could be bad eyesight, but likely isn't. He had a different axe to grind. Josephus wanted the lion attack to result in proper worship of God so that he could make a larger point about hating Samaritans. He called them "proselytes of lions," fair-weather worshipers of God who needed actual proof before they would have faith. And if you think Josephus bent over backwards on that one, you should see the commentators who try to make both interpretations work and go with "a plague of lions." For a chapter about how bad syncretism is, later commentators sure do indulge in a lot of it trying to drag this particular cart up the hill.

The Reverse Josephus Dodge—Instead of ignoring the text and saying the syncretic worship didn't happen, Marvin A. Sweeney interprets a lack of text to mean that the lions never stopped. Since the Bible doesn't specifically say the lions stopped, they must have kept on coming. Of course, it doesn't say they continued either. But, like the old saying goes: absence of evidence is not evidence of absence. Sweeney does admit the *deus terrae* problem exists, but tries to reframe it in the larger problem of the existence of evil. This doesn't help.

Sweeney also tries threading the needle by saying God didn't send lions. Instead, the lions, as God's creations, knew what they had to do and required no orders. But God created everything, right? Do we all have revenge orders waiting on us? Call it the mafia variation.

Meyer Appel goes all in and says lions can't be stopped without divine aid (since divine power sent them). He leaves the next premise to the imagination, but ultimately he must mean that the worship wasn't syncretic. If the lions stopped, God stopped them. And God is not down with syncretism. But again this contradicts the plain text.

The Depopulation Dodge—God didn't send lions, despite the explicit text. The mass resettlement emboldened lions to do what they do. This also solves nothing. Really, it's a form of the Historical Dodge. But it's particularly flawed because these commentators want to keep the theological interpretation. This one is really popular. Milton Terry adds that the Samarians were resettled in the cities, not the rural areas, further inviting the lions by man's absence. Even the Seventh Day Adventists go for this, deemphasizing God's role.

I am constantly amazed at commentators who will sell you on the Garden of Eden, but will try to play the realist when problems like this are pointed out. Denying God's role in this passage is a simple way to move past the *deus terrae* problem. If God didn't do anything directly, then there's no problem. Except for the plain text of the Bible.

Almost all of the other dodges have the Depopulation Dodge as a component, but these are the ones that went with it the hardest. W. L. Baxter even goes so far as to say **2 Kings** is "a fully informed and reliable history," trying to push the realistic interpretation of events. Adam Clarke calls the Samarians superstitious for thinking God sent lions, then says God definitely did send them. Johann Christoph Friedrich goes with the Depopulation Dodge, and adds that the lions didn't so much stop as taper off.

Gina Hens-Piazza writes that the Samarians are wrong in their assumption that God sent the lions, but the text says God sent lions. Otto Thenius goes with the Depopulation Dodge and slams Josephus for calling the lions a plague, as if that were the problem.

It has to be asked—were lions common in the area? It's hard to know for sure. Zoologists say that lions were once evenly distributed around the globe in the Late Holocene, but humans hunted them to extinction in many areas.[4] So, from a scientific point of view, it would have been unusual to see a lot of lions. Random sightings were noted until the Crusades.

The Isaiah Dodge—*No lion shall be there, nor any ravenous beast shall go up thereon, it shall not be found there; but the redeemed shall walk there.*— **Isaiah 35:9, NIV Edition**

We've all been at the business end of this kind of argument. The Bible verses start flying without context. This one attempts to flip the script by saying God doesn't send lions, he only removes lions. Jimmy Swaggart really likes this one, and Edward Lee Curtis did a whole paper on this.

They cite this as negative proof that the Samarians are in trouble with God. God didn't send lions, he stopped preventing their natural return. It's really passive-aggressive and is a weak effort to dilute the plain language of "God sent lions." Also, both sources really lean on the whole "mongrel race" thing, which is a bit of a tell.

The Historical Dodge—This is the claim that **1** and **2 Kings** are historical books, not theological ones. It casts the *deus terrae* problem as merely a flaw in the historical record and not a theological problem. So why include historical proof of a theological problem?

I. W. Slotki's wrinkle on this is to call the Samarians ignorant for thinking God sent the lions. He claims that all that's being described is the incorrect notions of the Samarians. Again, why include it at all?

The Literary Historical Dodge—Kings is a historical book and God is sometimes used as a rhetorical device, and is not meant to be a real actor in human events. *Deus terrae* is just a literary problem. Expecting God to behave consistently in the Bible is like expecting Spider-Man to be consistent from Ditko until now. After the Depopulation Dodge, this is probably the most popular move.

John Gray sees **2 Kings 17:24-28** as an insertion by "a local priestly authority." Suddenly anybody can slip something into the Bible. But this just supports my thesis. If the passage is an anomaly inserted by people who aren't on board with the rest of the Bible, why not remove it?

The more textual and historically-minded commentators also have their doubts about the passage. Shemaryu Talmon makes an interesting case for **2 Kings 17:25-26** being lifted from a separate historical record, one based out of Bethel. **2 Kings 17** as a whole, he says, is probably one of the last parts of **Kings** to be written, and it reflects a Judean bias. In other words, the story was included to bag on the Samaritans.

This is all well and good, but it doesn't help the theological ramifications, and strengthens the argument that the passage shouldn't be there. Pieter Willem van der Horst doubts the passage has any historical value at all. Many writers see this syncretism as the origins of the Samaritan religion, which may be why it is included.

John Skinner decides to go all the way with the Literary-Historical Dodge and says the editor of **2 Kings** included the lions story because he liked it, but didn't alter the text to fit the rest of the book. To claim in this one and only instance, in which an editor artlessly inserts a passage that says God sent lions, that the editor is being too historically accurate to make the theology work is sacrificing the integrity of the larger work to score a small point.

Richard D. Nelson notes a lack of narrative condemnation of the Bethel priest who presided over the syncretism. Therefore the narrator didn't really care about these events and got sloppy. Again—why include it?

Pauline A. Viviano, who wrote the only dissertation I could find about this passage, starts strong. She notes a ring pattern in the storytelling of **2 Kings**, and claims that the facts of this passage were altered to retain the ring construction. Because the ring construction was more important than the theology?

Reality starts to get really fuzzy with Bustenay Oded, who notes that, given what happens in the rest of the books of **Kings**, there should have been a prophet to warn the Samarians. But since the Samarians do not believe in prophets, they didn't get one. This works as a literary explanation for sure, and suggests the passage was by a later Judean author who wanted to sock it to the Samaritans. But this doesn't help anything. Volkmar Fritz goes down the same path.

Benisch wants to split hairs on whether the Samarians actually understood their troubles when the lions showed. But this interpretation means the King of Assyria somehow knew what the deal was and sent the Bethel priest, and that's a stretch.

The Nothing To See Here Dodge—The problem is ignored. Or they do something really radical. The author that seems the most cognizant of the *deus terrae* problem is Iain W. Provan. He ties himself in knots over it before starting the fatal sentence "If the reader mentally supplies quotation marks...".

Ultimately, he claims that the passage is ironically included, a straw man to be demolished by the rest of the book. You only *think* you read that God sent lions to attack people who then practiced syncretism and stopped being attacked. But it in fact means the opposite because...yeah. This is a serious hail mary. The passage doesn't fit Provan's vision, so the writers simply didn't mean that. I almost called this one the God Is Testing You Dodge.

The Assimilation Dodge—Michael M. Kaplan suggests that the story is like the later editions of the Bible used to win converts from other religions (like the *HELIAND* for the Saxons). This takes a bit of background. Lions are significant in Assyrian culture. They were present and real, yet had a touch of the divine. Any being in the running for apex predator is going to seem at least a little divine in its power. Assyrian contract law uses oaths like "May a lion eat my face if I break this covenant." And these are considered serious and legit, because a lion can be arranged if one party decides to breach the contract. Lions weren't used to literally enforce these contracts, but they were certainly more compelling fictional outcomes than "may God strike me down." But this explanation still leaves us with our initial problem intact, and only reinforces why lions were used.

The Tenant Dodge—Michael M. Kaplan also posits that God's covenant is literally with the land and not the people, except insofar as they may or may not live on that land. This suggests that the Israelites that resettled outside the Holy Land are off the hook. They can become Buddhists or Zoroastrians. And the people resettled to the Holy Land without so much as a truckstop tract to go by are bound by the original covenant. Maybe Moses should have left the Ten Commandments where they were, since they were more of a road sign than a portable creed. Also *THE CHRISTIAN'S COMPLETE FAMILY BIBLE* suggests that God was used to the warmth of worship from that area previously, and noticed when it was suddenly gone. They also suggest that the lions punished the Samarians on their own initiative—lions as mafia, like Sweeney's variation on the Depopulation Dodge.

The Refocus Dodge—Frazer uses this with enough success that he burns down the whole thing by taking it to its logical conclusion. All religions were local then, he writes. It's no surprise that the religion of Yahweh was the same. When religions went global culturally, so did their gods' domains.

This is absolutely correct and cannot be the position of Christians without admitting this passage is a problem reflecting an outdated religious view. If the Bible was considered an historical document instead of holy word, everything would be fine. But many Christians want to have their religion and their history as one, tacking from one to the other as needed in the moment. But the Bible is an imperfect document, and needs revision.

Spinoza is on my side on this one. He specifically points to this passage as a problem, using it to bolster his argument that these stories are not meant to be taken literally. But that doesn't let Spinoza off, really. He tries to go with the *when you look at the big picture*...that kind of argument. View it from an altitude where you can't make out the contours of the problem anymore. Bury the problem in the pages of a huge Bible commentary, for instance. But, even as parable, this story doesn't help the rest of the Bible in the slightest.

I ran across a fascinating article from *MISSIOLOGY: AN INTERNATIONAL REVIEW* by Jacob Loewe that cops to all of this. His focus was seeing the *deus terrae* (he doesn't use the term) as a faulty method of proselytizing. His assertion is that all other forms of worship must be purged from all peoples, thereby avoiding syncretism when bringing the word of God to people who already have a culture and traditions of their own.

And from there he goes into numerous examples of local religions and how similar they are to the "god of that country" notion in **2 Kings**. He ends up making the case for the *deus terrae* problem by approaching it from another direction. The R&D Department doesn't see it, but the folks in Sales know what's up.

The Newton's Apple (of Knowledge) Dodge—Literally used by Isaac Newton! The Samarians are punished because they knew better than to not worship God. He doesn't get into the racist erasure of the Jews stuff, so he can try this. This is bolstered by the Samarians realizing their mistake after the lion attack. Newton says God hates a Christian drunkard more than a drunkard. This is one of the better dodges, but it still doesn't escape the gravity of the *deus terrae* problem. It just reframes it as an epistemological problem instead of a geographical one. Only people who know better are punished? You have to buy into the system before it can punish you? Is this omnipotence and omniscience? It's an argument to ignore the whole process.

The Scheduling Dodge—*THE PREACHER'S COMPLETE HOMILETICAL COMMENTARY OF THE OLD TESTAMENT* really leans into the problem. "Not even the veriest Pagan can be excused for his ignorance of God." Then they suggest that it could happen anywhere else, so watch out. God will get to you at some point. But I have to give it to them. They are 100% sure it was God. "How much worse than Assyrians are they who are ready to ascribe all calamities to nature, to chance!"

But this highlights the *deus terrae* problem. It doesn't solve it, just because

God's a busy entity and hasn't gotten to sending lions to all the heathens yet.

The Lion Pandemic Dodge—Matthew Henry admits that God should send lions all over the world, but He waited for someone to come to His land to make the mistake of not worshiping Him. Everyone else has to find God on their own without the favor of a lion attack to get them moving. He also says "yet beside the natural cause, there was a manifest hand of God in it." That puts him in the Depopulation Dodge category, but the pirouette he does at the end warrants special mention.

The "AR Stands For Armalite Rifle" Dodge—Bodenheimer calls the whole thing into doubt because the Samarians and the writer of this passage were not zoologists. So they can't be trusted to discuss lion activity correctly. Then what was eating the Samarians? This dodge creates many more questions than it answers.

The "Dodge"—J. Glentworth Butler puts "the god of the land" in quotes and presses on as if that explains everything.

The WTF Dodge—My favorite commentator is predictably from the Internet. The Sixth Day Ministry has classic lines like "How could God send lions? Wouldn't He have to be in control of them?" Or this mind-bending extrapolation: "If God controls the lions, do you think he controls the white tails? What about the elk, turkey, squirrels, and waterfowl?" If God had sent squirrels to kill the Samarians, the depopulation guys would be in a real pickle.

Why can't commentators leave **2 Kings 17:25-26** alone? It's a statement that, presented alone, seems like a normal line of the Bible. God does all kinds of things, and no small amount of killing. But a lot of writers seek to remove God's agency from a line in the Bible that reads "God sent lions among them." And what does removing God's agency from the Bible do for anyone?

V. The Solution

The answer to the *deus terrae* problem is simple: strike **2 Kings 17:25-26**. Just those lines. No authority is challenged by this. Even the racists get to have their party, which proves how fair this is. I bet the Pope wouldn't care.

It will be said of me that I mean to do violence to the Bible, by demanding a passage be cut. But this violence happens regularly. Many popular Bibles are published in magazine format to draw in young readers. And they leave some things out and pretend it's complete. People from all sects want some parts gone, or at least forgotten or omitted. Bible study is largely treated as if it's pass/fail anyway. Long as you get enough of it, you're good to go.

Besides, if I wanted to make mischief, I'd say something like—I could tell you that the Qabbalaistic value of "lion" and "vampire" are the same. But who means every word they write and say? Isn't it just as possible that they wrote "lion" and meant "vampire?" Have you never written something, reviewed it a hundred times and then someone shows you an error? Are they errors? Or is it a means of divination by elimination, a trance where the unconscious protects its contributions? I can do that stuff all day.

There's a real fear with revising the Bible. Many have done it and created their own versions. Hell, **2 Kings** used to be **4 Kings**. But the central text remains. No one major religion controls the text, but none of the major religions are willing to try changing it. Because it always results in fragmentation of the flock. Some folks will not accept any change in the Bible, because they believe it to be the word of God, even the parts that don't work. But why let this stuff bog you down?

Kings as a whole stays because of the prophets. That's why the Depopulation Dodge is so common among commentators. They don't know what this story is doing here, either. The pattern of **Kings** is 1) people are bad, 2) prophet shows up to warn them they're bad, 3) people ignore prophet, 4) mayhem ensues. **2 Kings 17:25-26** skips steps 2 and 3. And it's not much of a story. But what is, when you have characters like Elijah storming around?

Deleting **2 Kings 17:25-26** neatly solves the *deus terrae* problem. You can say that I am solving a problem I created, but that is academia in a nutshell, friends. Now I can hear some folks saying *but you're leaving in one of the "god of that country" references, John.* Glad you asked. In the *NEW JITV VERSION* **2 Kings 17** will read like this:

The king of Assyria brought people from Babylon, Kuthah, Avva, Hamath and Sepharvaim and settled them in the towns of Samaria to replace the Israelites. They took over Samaria and lived in its towns. Then the king of Assyria gave this order: "Have one of the priests you took captive from Samaria go back to live there and teach the people what the god of the land requires." So one of the priests who had been exiled from Samaria came to live in Bethel and taught them how to worship the Lord.

Now the passage reads as if the "god of that country" reference is a derogatory statement by the King of Assyria about the religion of the area. This lets the Historical-Literary dodgers be right, because that's how it would read in the new context. You're welcome.

It also pins the blame for the syncretism on the king. Maybe that was his goal all along. The sinister king introduces syncretism under the guise of praising a local god. It sets up the later punishments in **2 Kings** and provides a proper villain. Plus, if you want to keep up the vendetta against the Samaritan religion, the way is clear.

It also creates room for speculation on motives for sending the priest. The now-apocryphal lines 25 and 26 can still be used by scholars if they really want to reopen that can of worms. But my guess is, they won't. They'll be glad to be rid of the problem.

Probably some historians will want to keep it, but the problem here isn't one of history. It's a problem of theology. So they can pretend it's still there and write think pieces on why churches removed the line. This solution is a scholarly paper machine. CV's will swell all over the world. Baby steps toward tenure will be assured.

VI. Removal Methods

It all starts with a single step. *THE NEW JITV VERSION* of the Bible is licensed under Creative Commons and is available for free at dativebooks.com. We just need to spread it around. This version is free to all. If you change it, change the name to something else. "Based on the *NEW JITV VERSION* text" will do just fine.

If you want to help, post the edition on your site. Get Bible Gateway to link to it. Quote it whenever you quote the Bible. Whatever. You can even denounce it. All that matters is that it's a version of the Bible that's out in the world.

Give ear, ye heavens, and I will speak;
And let the earth hear the words of my mouth.
My doctrine shall drop as the rain;
My speech shall distil as the dew,
As the small rain upon the tender grass,
And as the showers upon the herb.

—Deuteronomy 32:1-2, *NEW JITV VERSION*

VII. Postscript

Before I fling the whole bibliography at you, I have one more thing to show. I did a lot of the reading for this article at conventions, as there's often a lot of downtime for writers. And looking busy tends to draw traffic. Occasionally I'd do some Jitting as I read. So here's some of that. I have blurred out the articles themselves, because JSTOR and Elsevier will depopulate your wallet if you mess with them.

Endnotes

1	Their argument goes like this. Once they were removed from the land, they weren't special anymore. Plus they intermarried with the locals in their new home, and you get the picture. They use phrases like "mongrel people" and have a big party. At the other end of this continuum, there has been a lot of debate as to whether Samaritans are Jews. The Samaritans built their own temple at Mt. Gerizim because Alexander the Great couldn't give a fraction of a damn either way and a rift formed in Judaism. And this only got worse. The Samaritans believe that only the Pentateuch is the actual word of God. They reject all other parts of what we know as the Bible, especially prophets.

2	I use "Samarian" throughout because that's an inhabitant of Samaria. "Samaritans" refers to the creed and not the people as a whole.

3	Sargon mentions conquering the Samarians in his annals, but picture this—there is some scholarly disagreement. I have no dog in this hunt, so I'm going with the guy with textual support. But if you're a Shalmaneser or an Esarhaddon person, what I have to say doesn't rely on this.

4	Soon it'll be all areas, if we don't stop the industry that lets rich jags shoot them from armored trucks in a vain attempt to look like a real hunter.

BIBLIOGRAPHY

"It was the lions, the lions, the lions, the lions!"—C. H. Spurgeon.

Nothing To See Here Dodgers

Clarke, Adam. *The Holy Bible, Containing the Old and New Testaments : The Text Printed from the Most Correct Copies of the Present Authorized Translation, including the Marginal Readings and Parallel Texts : With a Commentary and Critical Notes, Designed as a Help to a Better Understanding of the Sacred Writings.* Super Royal Octavo Stereotype ed. Cincinnati: Applegate, 1854.

Knoppers, Gary N. "Cutheans or Children of Jacob? The Issue of Samaritan Origins in 2 Kings 17." *Reflection and Refraction,* vol. 113, 2007, pp. 223–239. Vetus Testamentum, Supplements.

Nichol, Francis David. *The Seventh-Day Adventist Bible Commentary.* Washington DC: Review and Herald Publishing Association. 1953.

Provan, I. *1 & 2 Kings.* Sheffield, England: Sheffield Academic Press. 1997.

Talmon, S. "Polemics and apology in biblical historiography; 2 Kings 17:24-41." In *The Creation of Sacred Literature.* Berkeley: U of California Press. 1981.

Urquhart, John. *The New Biblical Guide.* Marshall Brothers, 1898.

Josephus Dodgers

The Compendious Commentary. The Holy Bible, with comm. by J. R. McGavin. United Kingdom, n.p, 1861.

Chrysostom, St. John. *The Homilies of S. John Chrysostom, Archbishop of Constantinople, on the Gospel of St. John.* Oxford: J. H. Parker. 1848.

Friedrich, J. Christoph. *Discussionum de Christologia Samaritanorum liber: accedit appendicula de columba dea Samaritarum.* Lipsiae: In Libraria Weidmannia. 1821.

Josephus, Flavius, Maynard, G., & Kimpton, E. *The whole genuine and complete works of Flavious [sic] Josephus : To which is added various youthful indexes ... : Also, a continuation of the history of the Jews, from Josephus down to the present time....* New York: Printed by W. Durell, for Bell & Smith, booksellers & stationers, corner of Magazine and Chatham Streets. 1799.

Lange, Johann Peter. *A Commentary on the Holy Scriptures: Critical, Doctrinal, and Homilectical, with Special Reference to Ministers and Students.* United States, C. Scribner & Company, 1890.

Reverse-Josephus Dodgers

Appel, M. *Quaestiones de rebus Samaritanorum sub imperio Romanorum peractis.* Gottingae: In libraria Dieterichiana. 1874.

Sweeney, Marvin A. *I & II Kings.* Presbyterian Publishing Corporation, 2007.

Isaiah Dodgers

Curtis, Edward Lewis. "Isaiah's Prophecy Concerning the Shoot

of Jesse and His Kingdom: Isaiah XI." *The Old & New Testament Student*, vol. 12, no. 1, 1891, pp. 13–19.

The Interpreter's Bible: The Holy Scriptures in the King James and Revised Standard Versions...In Twelve Volumes. United States, Abingdon-Cokesbury, 1990.

Jimmy Swaggart Bible Commentary: I Kings, II Kings. United States, World Evangelism Press, 2011.

Historical-Literary Dodgers

Benisch, A. (Abraham). *Jewish School and Family Bible*. London: James Darling.

Cogan, et al. *II Kings : a New Translation / with Introduction and Commentary by Mordechai Cogan and Hayim Tadmor*. First ed., Doubleday, 1988.

Fritz, Volkmar. *1 & 2 Kings / Volkmar Fritz ; Translated by Anselm Hagedorn*. First English language ed., Fortress, 2003.

Hobbs, T. R. *2 Kings*. Word Books, 1985.

Keil, Carl Friedrich. *The Books of the Kings*, tr. by J. Martin. United Kingdom, n.p, 1872.

Nelson, Richard D. *First and Second Kings. Interpretation, a Bible Commentary for Teaching and Preaching*. Atlanta: John Knox Press, 1987.

Oded, Bustanay. "II Kings 17: Between History and Polemic." *Jewish History*, vol. 2, no. 2, 1987, pp. 37–50.

Skinner, Rev. Professor. *The New Century Bible: Kings*. Edinburgh [etc.]: T. C. & E. C. Jack, 1904.

Viviano, Pauline A. "2 Kings 17: A Rhetorical and Form-Critical Analysis." *The Catholic Biblical Quarterly*, vol. 49, no. 4, 1987, pp. 548–559.

Depopulation Dodgers

Butler, James Glentworth. *The Bible-work: the Old Testament*. New York: Funk and Wagnals. 1898.

Cobbin, Ingram. *The Condensed Commentary and Family Exposition of the Holy Bible....* United Kingdom, Thomas Ward and Company, 27 Paternoster Row, 1837.

Friedrich, J. Christoph. *Discussionum de Christologia Samaritanorum liber: accedit appendicula de columba dea Samaritarum*. Lipsiae: In Libraria Weidmannia. 1821.

Grieve, A. J. (Alexander James)., Peake, A. S. (Arthur Samuel). *A Commentary on the Bible*. New York: T. Nelson. 1919.

Henry, Matthew. *An exposition of all the books of the Old and New Testaments: ...: Wherein each chapter is summed up in its contents: the sacred text inserted at large in distinct paragraphs ... largely illustrated with practical remarks and observations..* Berwick-up-on-Tweed,: Printed by and for W. Gracie. 1808.

Hens-Piazza, Gina. *Abingdon Old Testament Commentaries | 1-2 Kings]*. United Kingdom, Abingdon Press, 2006.

Lumby, J. Rawson. *The Second Book of the Kings / Edited by the Rev. J. Rawson Lumby*. University Press, 1914.

Slotki, I. W. *Kings: Hebrew Text & English Translation / with an Introd. and Commentary by I. W. Slotki*. First ed., Soncino Press, 1950.

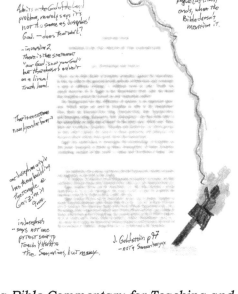

Terry, Milton S. *Commentary on the Old Testament...: Kings to Esther*. United States, Phillips & Hunt, 1875.

Thenius, Otto. *Die Bücher der Könige*. Germany, Hirzel, 1873.

Vermigli, P., Froschauer, Christoph, & Wolf, Johann. *Melachim, id est, Regum libri duo posteriores cum Commentarijs*. Escudebat Christophorus Froschouerus. 1571.

Refocus Dodgers

Frazer, James George. *Folk-lore in the Old Testament: Studies in Comparative Religion, Legend and Law*. United Kingdom, Macmillan and Company, limited, 1919.

Spinoza, Benedictus de. *A Spinoza Reader: The Ethics and Other Works*. United States, Princeton University Press, 2020.

Scheduling Dodger

The Preacher's Complete Homiletical Commentary: (on an original plan). Funk & Wagnalls company. 1892.

AR Stands For Armalite Dodger

Bodenheimer, Friedrich Simon. *Animal and Man in Bible Lands*. Netherlands, E. J. Brill, 1960.

The Newton's Apple (of Knowledge) Dodger

Newton, Isaac. Babson Ms. 437. www.newtonproject.ox.ac.uk. 2005.

Tenant Dodger

Kaplan, Michael Matthew. *The Lion In The Hebrew Bible: A Study Of A Biblical Metaphor*, 1981.

The Christian's Complete Family Bible: Containing The Whole Of The Sacred Text Of The Old And New Testaments, With The Apocrypha At Large. Bolton [Lancashire]: B. Jackson. 1790.

WTF Dodger

Barnett, D. "II Kings 17:25-26." "Hunting for Eternity", Sixth Day Outdoor Ministry, 17 Sept. 2018, sixthdayom.com/2018/09/17/ii-kings-1725-26/.

The Rest

Biblia sacra latina Veteris Testamenti Hieronymo interprete ex antiquissima auctoritate in stiches descripta...Ed. instituit suasore Christ. Carolo Iosia de Bunsen, Theodorus Heyse, ad finem perduxit Constantinus de Tischendorf.... Lipsiae: F. A. Brockhaus. 1873.

The English Version of the Polyglott Bible, Containing the Old and New Testaments: With the Marginal Readings : A Copious and Original Selection of References to Parallel and Illustrative Passages, Exhibited in a Manner Hitherto Unattempted. C. Wells. 1843.

*The Hexaglot Bible: Comprising the Holy Scriptures of the Old and New Testaments in the Original Tongues, Together with the Septuagint, the Syriac (of the New Testament), the Vulgate, the Authorized English, and German, and the Most Approved French Versions; Arranged in Parallel Columns....*United States, Funk and Wagnalls, 1901.

"The History Of The New...Confirmed And Illustrated By

Passages Of Josephus, The Jewish Historian." *Religious Monitor, and Evangelical Repository*, vol. 8, no. 6, 1831, p. 355_356.

The Holy Bible: Containing the Old and New Testaments and the Apocrypha. Boston: R. H. Hinkley, 1904.

Barnett, Ross, et al. "Phylogeography of Lions (Panthera Leo Ssp.) Reveals Three Distinct Taxa and a Late Pleistocene Reduction in Genetic Diversity." *Molecular Ecology*, vol. 18, no. 8, 2009, pp. 1668–1677.

Barnett, Ross, et al. "Revealing the Maternal Demographic History of Panthera Leo Using Ancient DNA and a Spatially Explicit Genealogical Analysis." *BMC Evolutionary Biology*, vol. 14, no. 1, 2014, p. 70.

Barton, Muddiman, Barton, John, and Muddiman, John. *The Oxford Bible Commentary.* New York: Oxford University Press, 2001.

Brown, et al. *The Jerome Biblical Commentary.* Prentice Hall, 1968.

Cheyne, T. K. (Thomas Kelly). *Critica biblica: or, Critical notes on the text of the Old Testament writings....* London: A. and C. Black. 1904.

Clarke, A. *Holy Bible...With A Commentary And Critical Notes.* Baltimore. 1834.

Cohn, Robert L. "The Literary Structure of Kings." In *The Books of Kings.* pp107-122. 2010.

Conant, Thomas Jefferson, and American Baptist Publication Society. *The Books of Joshua, Judges, Ruth, I and II Samuel, I and II Kings: The Common Version Revised.* American Baptist Publication Society, 1884.

Davidson, Samuel. *The Canon of the Bible: Its Formation, History, and Fluctuations.* C. Kegan Paul, 1878.

Ellicott, C. J. (Charles John). *An Old Testament Commentary For English Readers.* London: Cassell, Petter, Galpin & Co. 1884.

Geikie, Cunningham. *Hours with the Bible; Or, The Scriptures in the Light of Modern Discovery and Knowledge.* J. Pott, 1882.

Gray, John. *I & II Kings : Commentary.* Second, Fully Revised ed. Old Testament Library. London: S.C.M. Press, 1970.

Holland, Drew. "The Form and Function of the Source Citations in 1–2 Kings." *Zeitschrift Für Die Alttestamentliche Wissenschaft* 130, no. 4 (2018): 559-570.

Horst, P. "Samaritan origins according to the 'Paralipomena Jeremiae'." In *Studies in Ancient Judaism and Early Christianity*, pp161-172. 2014.

Jahn, J., Stowe, C. E. (Calvin Ellis). *Jahn's History Of The Hebrew Commonwealth.* Andover: Printed by Flagg and Gould for G. & C. Carvill. 1828.

Jamieson, Fausset, Brown, Fausset, A. R., and Brown, David. *A Commentary, Critical and Explanatory, on the Old and New Testaments.* Hartford, Conn.: S. S. Scranton, 1875.

Kartveit, Magnar. "4. Josephus On The Origin Of The Samaritans." In *The Origin of the Samaritans*, 71-108. Vol. 128. Vetus Testamentum, Supplements. 2009.

Kartveit, Magnar. "Anti-Samaritan polemics in the Hebrew Bible? : The case of 2 Kings 17:24-41." *Studia Judaica,*

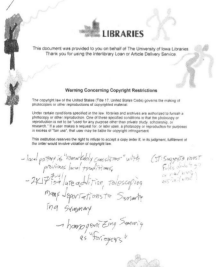

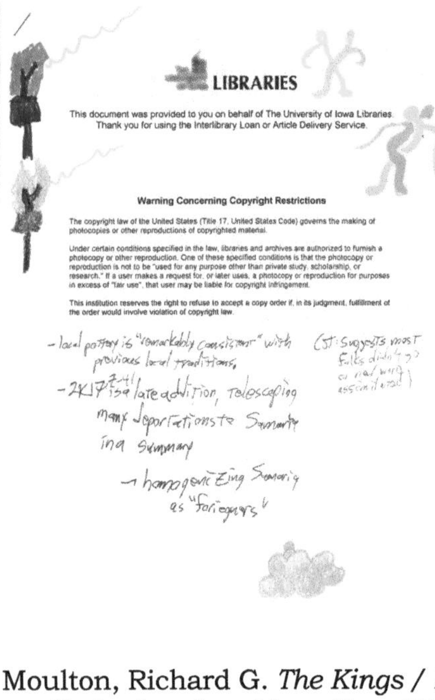
LIBRARIES

This document was provided to you on behalf of The University of Iowa Libraries.
Thank you for using the Interlibrary Loan or Article Delivery Service.

Warning Concerning Copyright Restrictions

The copyright law of the United States (Title 17, United States Code) governs the making of photocopies or other reproductions of copyrighted material.

Under certain conditions specified in the law, libraries and archives are authorized to furnish a photocopy or other reproduction. One of these specified conditions is that the photocopy or reproduction is not to be "used for any purpose other than private study, scholarship, or research." If a user makes a request for, or later uses, a photocopy or reproduction for purposes in excess of "fair use", that user may be liable for copyright infringement.

This institution reserves the right to refuse to accept a copy order if, in its judgment, fulfillment of the order would involve violation of copyright law.

- local pottery is "remarkably consistent" with previous local traditions,
- 2K17:24-41 is a late addition, telescoping many deportations to Samaria in a summary
→ homogenizing Samaria as "foriegners"

(JT: suggests most folks didn't go …)

3-18. 2018.

Kartveit, Magnar. "The Date of II Reg 17, 24-41." *Zeitschrift Fur Die Alttestamentliche Wissenschaft*, 126(1), 31-44. 2014.

Kretzmann, P. *Popular Commentary Of The Bible : The Old Testament*. St. Louis: Concordia Publishing House. 1923.

Lightfoot, John. *The Whole Works Of The Late Rev. John Lightfoot....* London: Printed for G. Cowie and Co. 1823.

Lobstein, Joan. Mich. *Commentatio Historico-Philologica de Montibus Ebal & Garizim. Journal Des Savants*, 70(13), 40. 1773.

Loewen, Jacob. "Which God Do Missionaries Preach?" *Missiology*, vol. 14, no. 1, 1986, pp. 3–19.

Merrill, Stephen. *A Harmony of the Kings and Prophets: Or, An Arrangement of the History Contained in the Books of Kings and Chronicles, Together with the Writings of the Prophets Introduced in Chronological Order as They Were Delivered, Commencing with the Revolt of the Ten Tribes , and Closing with the Prophecy of Malachi.* Sabbath School Society, 1832.

Moulton, Richard G. *The Kings / Ed. with an Introduction and Notes.* Modern Reader's Bible. New York : London: Macmillan, Macmillan &, 1897.

Olley, John W. *The Message of Kings.* United Kingdom, InterVarsity Press, 2016.

Olmstead, A. T. "The Fall of Samaria." *The American Journal of Semitic Languages and Literatures* 21, no. 3 (1905): 179-82.

Porter, John Scott, Smith, George Vance, and Wellbeloved, Charles. *The Holy Scriptures of the Old Covenant in a Revised Translation.* Longman, Brown, Green, Longmans and Roberts, 1859.

Robertson, James. *The First and Second Books of Kings.* J. M. Dent: J. B. Lippincott, 1902.

Rosel, Hartmut N. "Why 2 Kings Does Not Constitute a Chapter of Reflection in the "deuteronomistic History"." *Journal of Biblical Literature* 128, no. 1 (2009): 85-90.

Schnitzler, Annik E. "Past and Present Distribution of the North African–Asian Lion Subgroup: a Review." *Mammal Review*, vol. 41, no. 3, 2011, pp. 220–243.

Spurgeon, C. H. *Sham Conversion.* 1905. https://www.spurgeongems.org/sermon/chs2928.pdf

Strawn, Brent A. *What Is Stronger than a Lion? Leonine Image and Metaphor in the Hebrew Bible and the Ancient Near East.* Academic Press / Vandenhoeck & Ruprecht, 2005.

Swete, Henry Barclay. *The Old Testament in Greek, According to the Septuagint.* University Press, 1895.

Tanner, Joseph Marion, and Deseret Sunday School Union. *Old Testament Studies.* Deseret Sunday School Union, 1917.

Whaley, Ernest Boyd. *Samaria and the Samaritans in Josephus's "Antiquities" 1-11*, 1989.

Whedon, D. D, and Terry, Milton Spenser. *Kings to Esther.* Hunt & Eaton: Cranston & Stowe, 1875.

Wright, William Aldis. *The Authorised Version of the English Bible, 1611.* Cambridge English Classics. Cambridge: University Press, 1909.

Younger, K. "The repopulation of Samaria (2 Kings 17:24, 27-31) in light of recent study." In *The Future of Biblical Archaeology* pp. 254-280. 2004.

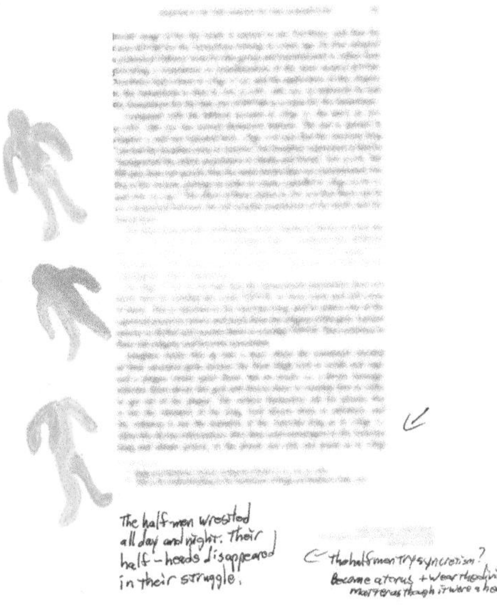
The half-men wrestled all day and night. Their half-heads disappeared in their struggle.
The half men try syncretism? Became a torus + wear the divine matter as though it were a head?

With the advent of Big Data, we have a new predictive method reaching mainstream status. Mass reactions are used to calculate future results, with outliers not only registered, but used to prove their opposite. Yet all that data crunching has done is succeed in making us madder at each other.

Big Data is scrying—people as tea leaves, people as stars. When Big Data fails to predict, it blames the data, using truisms about logic and computers (garbage in, garbage out) as legitimacy drag.

Blaming the data makes you look smarter. Blaming the believer's insufficient faith works similarly. But it's not our motives that matter.

We are ourselves thoughts, interacting in prescribed ways. Our lives are programs, the patterns within them the very code that determines what we can and should do. We are the neural impulses of a giant brain. We do not have thoughts of our own. We interact, as quarks do to make a rock, to serve a purpose beyond our scope. Why does history repeat itself? Because our parameters, our computed values, make it inevitable.

Adel HOYT-KELL

already knows what you're thinking.

#118 on card

This does not present an answer to the question of a determined universe. The fact that the programming in an ATM makes it spit out money when you put the right card and code in doesn't make this a deterministic universe. For our programmers, for the being that benefits from our combined interactions, the universe is free and random. We do not live lives. We execute the program. We process until we die and more replace us.

But here's the good news. Morality is pointless! Our actions have no more moral value than one skin cell replacing another. We do not call it murder when new cells supplant the old. We don't even call it murder when a virus invades and rewires a cell, erasing its former self. We don't even call it slavery. It's just a process, and that's all we are.

I know what you're thinking. Adel just threw off the shackles of society and declared our lives to be meaningless. Might as well go stab somebody. But you won't. And it's not because you aren't convinced of what I'm saying. The pull of your programming will keep you behaving just as you did before.

We are not only our programming. We have randomizing elements in us that our programming has no opinion about. This freedom makes us as curious to the larger entities as particles seem to us. The larger entity may even be aware of our existence in some abstract way. Since it is highly unlikely that it would remotely look like us, it would see biological life as an abstract possibility only.

So, I hear you mutter as you flip the page, what are we to do with this knowledge? Thanks for telling me my life is pointless and devoid of the moral value assigned to sentient life. There is room to move within this program.

Acting in concert, we can provoke changes in the larger entity. Given our regularity and general predictability, we must be part of the larger entity's autonomic system—breathing, heart rate, whatever passes for the unconscious business of living. It explains our relative freedom to act in other areas, such as aesthetic preferences. Our job is not difficult. We've even managed to dress our work in the cloak of free will. And we can use these choices to manipulate the program.

Imagine if everyone's favorite color were now yellow, to the exclusion of all other manufactured colors. What if we only listened to trip hop? Or only read furniture assembly instructions? We could change the program!

Our changes would ripple to the macro level of the larger entity, make it aware that we are here. It cannot simply think us away any more than our own unwanted thoughts can be unthought. We can affect the mental health of the larger entity to send our message.

There are risks. My own research suggests that the lack of life similar to our own in the universe may mean that we are the only thoughts the larger entity has. And if we are the autonomic system, the larger entity may be near brain death.

So, I know what you're thinking. Adel went from telling me I have no moral value to telling me that I'm a neural impulse in a dying galaxy brain. I have no value and what existence I have serves only to push blood through the veins of a comatose giant. I'm not even the thought it forms to take a piss. Do you do parties?

There are other possibilities. Life exists in many forms, as we know it. We're carbon-based, but there are sulfur-based bacteria in vents at the bottom of the ocean. It's possible that they're the autonomic system and we're something higher. It's possible that the myriad ways life can exist represent the full range of thoughts in the larger entity's brain.

But the only way to know for sure is to deliver a shock, a measurable jolt, to the larger entity. And we do that by working together. It may only take a few dozen, a few hundred, a few thousand people assembling yellow furniture while listening to *MEZZANINE* on a loop. We may already be having an effect. Look how much the world has changed lately.

It may not even be a numbers game. Maybe we should be listening to *DUMMY*. Maybe *PSYENCE FICTION*. Without continued research, we can't know for sure.

I know what you're thinking. What happens when we affect the larger entity? At best, it'll think it has lost its mind. And even if it ends up realizing its own neuron firings are individuals with souls and thoughts of their own, what's it supposed to do with that knowledge? Well, the good news is—I could be wrong.

Told you I knew what you were thinking.

There are always some Jitters who wish to have contact with me without also alerting me to the fact of their belief that I drew something important to them when I was nine. They will not engage me directly, even when I give unambiguous opportunities to do so. They do not buy my books. They flee when confronted or recognized.

What follows is an attempt to get something out of me by subterfuge. I've developed a pretty good sense for when I'm being probed by Jitters, but sometimes a well-developed sense looks too hard at the subtleties and misses the big picture. And sometimes I'm just a dumbass.

My guess is this brand of Jitter is trying to make lightning strike twice by steering me toward Jitting the way it originally happened—organically, with no intent. The Sunday school teacher didn't intend for me to draw what I did. Until I got the assignment, I didn't even know I'd be drawing that day.

It explains the subterfuge, but it's ultimately a flawed approach. The Jitters can't create a lack of intent. They have the intent. The process is tainted the second they decide to act.

THE JIT

is filling a bit of space with Jitter tricks.

#179 on card

I admire the effort, but would it kill you Jitters to buy the damn books? Not profiting from my religion puts me literally alone among religious figures in this country. If I told you I need a jet to spread the word about Jitting, would that work? How about a Winnebago? A skateboard? Why must the JIT be untainted by money?

Come to think of it, Whitney doesn't make anything either, does he? He does ad swaps in his zine, probably swaps the actual zines. I'm not at all clear on how he supports himself. Are you Jitters torturing him too? Or are you still ignoring him? How is it that Whitney and I are essentially treated the same by the Jitters? Are we both irrelevant? Both relevant? I'm kidding. Nobody pretends to be a parking industry magazine to interview Whitney.

The Jitter in this case actually does write for a parking industry magazine, and they really ran the interview. This is an article for the April 2009 issue of *BETWEEN THE LINES*, a parking industry journal that mostly concerns itself with the beauty of parking structures and touchless transactions. They profile parking professionals from all levels.

It looks like I brought up lions, the way they wrote it. But that was the closest they could get me to talk about any of it without setting off an alarm. Also, my work wasn't very happy that I talked about the worst of customers. It's considered a faux pas in customer service to admit that there are terrible people out there. That's really the job of reality shows.

THE *PRO* FILE

John Ira Thomas
The University of Iowa
Parking and Transportation

Dealing with angry calls keeps you on your toes, and John Ira Thomas has been on his for ten years.

"Have you ever gotten out of a moving car? then you're parked. End of story."

Normal people don't call parking offices. They've just received a ticket, or they want to address some small grievance writ large by other factors. Something terrible has happened and they want to blow up over something in scale with normal life. Whatever the reason, John Ira Thomas is at the other end of that phone. And he's heard it all. BETWEEN THE LINES caught up with Mr. Thomas to see what life is like in the front lines of parking.

Anonymity Breeds Cruelty

"It's just like the Internet out there. People think a phone is an anonymizer that insulates them from needing good manners when calling the parking office. I had a lady tell me one time...she claimed we didn't run buses to our biggest commuter lot after noon. I explained we run buses until midnight and she says 'I hope you have a wife and child and I hope they both get raped.' Who talks like that? I picture these people leveling threats at fast food workers. 'This ketchup isn't savory. I'll have your job for this.' You can get calls from nice people. It happens. But if you're not ready for someone with an emotional suicide vest calling you up and demanding your family be raped, you won't last long in this job."

Knowledge Is Power

"It's important that you stay on top of the details on your facilities. People will call and claim a sign you can see on the video feed isn't there. They're just trying to ice you, hoping it's your first day and they can sell you on the idea that your entire system is somehow fatally flawed and that this flaw was just discovered today. Because the alternative is that they're wrong, and they can't countenance that. They assume that they always behave correctly, so any ticket given to them is the result of malfeasance, trickery, or ninja activity. This iron grip on the feeling of their own infallibility forces them to invent completely absurd conclusions."

Reductio Ad Absurdum

"The best way to deal with them is to lead them further down the road they've chosen. Okay, we're all ninjas who appear in puffs of smoke to hand out expired meter tickets. You caught us. And?"

Speed Round

What animal are you most like?
"I dunno. A lion that eats dumb arguments and poops justice."

Are you religious?
"About as religious as someone who regularly loses faith in common sense can be."

And what does a lion that covets common sense believe?
"I really don't know what I expect anymore. I stopped hearing new arguments 9 years and 11 months ago."

Do you believe people can find their common sense again?
"Consensus reality checked out years ago. We have to relearn how to agree."

These next things are from the Spring 1991 *UNIVERSE'S LARGEST VIDEO PHENOMENA CATALOG*, a 78 page letter-size zine of eyesight-destroying type offering VHS dupes of all manner of TV and home-shot oddities. Imagine YouTube, only you pay or swap for 30-60 minute clips. Mostly these were UFO sightings and proofs of government conspiracy.

When I see these things on eBay, money dances out of my pocket. The joys of these catalogs approach the infinite. But when I saw these entries, I almost dropped this one in the toilet.

```
3/33/1991 @ 3:31 am        THE UNIVERSE'S LARGEST PHENOMENA CATALOG
Category Description Number Audio/Video (C/V) Product Number Subject Matter Approx. Time Date Rec.
17   V   7211C    Twin Forks Bigfoot Sighting                              88   4/06/1987 **
17   V   7211D    SUPERPOSITION!: El Chupacabra as Dimesional Traveler     30   6/16/1987 ****
17   V   7212     SIGHTINGS: Fouke Monster, Jersey Devil, Ogopogo, JIT     40   8/12/1987 ***
```

I can't find a JIT reference in any Bigfoot reference I own, and I'm a pretty large Bigfoot fan. It might be a coincidental regional name similarity, but damned if I know what it is. But it might be footage of me walking around, too.

I have scoured the internet looking for this video, and the best I can find is one that claims that the Fouke Monster and the Jersey Devil are the Ogopogo's parents, which is dumb because Ogopogo is a sea monster. Know your monsters, people.

```
3/33/1991 @ 3:31 am        THE UNIVERSE'S LARGEST PHENOMENA CATALOG
Category Description Number Audio/Video (C/V) Product Number Subject Matter Approx. Time Date Rec.
23   V   3156    How Many Presidents Were Never President At All?   58   1/03/1989 *****
23   V   3157    ALLEN DULLES: The Lion or The King?                89   4/20/1989 ***
23   V   3158    FACT AND FALLACY: The Anti-JIT                     19   5/05/1989 ***
```

These two just seem like trolling. Maybe the Allen Dulles thing is a coincidence, but a nineteen minute TV show about the Anti-JIT? It's gotta be public access TV, the great unarchived wilderness, lost to time.

In *PSYCHOPATHIA SEXUALIS,* there's a case of a nun driven over the edge wondering where Jesus' foreskin went. She couldn't think about anything else. *FACT AND FALLACY: The Anti-JIT* is my Jesus' foreskin.

I know what you're thinking. It wasn't Whitney. And the proof is simple. He would have bragged about it. And he doesn't think I made it up, or he would have denounced it. I think that means he's seen it. So it's real. And if he hasn't seen or heard of it until now, we'll know soon enough.

Searching YouTube now for this stuff yields only tiny nuggets like how JIT is Orlando slang for someone younger than you (but someone a lot younger is a JITterbug). It's also a dance in Detroit. But mostly you find a lot of videos about Just In Time inventory control.

There are also a lot of videos about Just In Time compiling, which involves compiling code at the time of program execution. And if I start another sentence pretending I have the slightest idea how that works, I'm already well out of knowledge about it. But they do call the act of coding this way "jitting." Regardless, the dance videos are much better.

If you search for Anti-JIT you get some Russian videos from a big fan of *SAW.* They're disorienting in that classic early Internet style. I don't think I received any subliminal orders from them, but your mileage may vary.

Do you feel you aren't moral enough? Do ethics make you feel like you're already behind in your quest to become a good person? Have you read an ethical treatise? What a headache! The philosophers and preachers and scolds of the world all write books that feel like they don't know the answers, because they don't!

There is no final form to moral and ethics. The scope of behavior and the reach of future technologies keep growing. Our knowledge of the sub-atomic world around us is so lacking that we may be doing incalculable harm to its denizens just by breathing. We don't need a creed, we need the triangle!

I live in a city whose logo is an asymmetrical pyramid. And one day I realized that it represented the relative distance of three defining points of morals—Legitima, Oujai, and Mishpat. These are terms from different ages, carefully chosen and arranged on the pyramid to define the zone of morality. If you can place your acts inside the pyramid, you're in the moral ballpark. And the closer you can place it to the infinite center of the pyramid? Well that means you're approaching true morality.

This isn't a game where you change definitions to cheat your way in. You can learn to honestly place acts relative to the three core concepts. I can show you.

An act is Legitima if it conforms to the written laws, not only of your country, state, and city. If you belong to a club that has bylaws, it means those too. Legitima is conformity to the written rules to which you are subject.

MARATHON JOSHI

is a Classicist with a plan for your life.

#191 on card

An act is Oujai if it brings you a sense of wellness and divinity. If an act gives you a feeling of spiritual and physical fullness, it is Oujai. If an act heals your psyche, amends are made, debts paid, it is Oujai.

An act is Mishpat if it conforms to the unspoken rules of the world, society, or even a friendship. An act is Mishpat if it fits the norms under which you live. Mishpat is more than common sense, but less than a written rule.

But what if you live in a place with terrible norms, like a prison or a frat house? What if what makes you feel good is hurting others needlessly? What if your land's laws are cruel and unjust? LOM is more than the sum of its parts. The Mishpat of prison can be mitigated or overcome by steering acts toward Oujai (finding mental peace) and Legitima (staying out of trouble with the guards). The Oujai of the psychopath can be overcome by Mishpat (social acceptance) and Legitima (the laws against harming others). The Legitima of cash bail and anti-trans laws can be defeated with Mishpat (organized resistance) and Oujai (the desire to make the laws better).

This moral system not only accepts that its tenets can be inverted and used for evil, it depends on it. By defining evil in moral terms, we can see what adjustments must be made to bring acts back into the pyramid. By learning how to apply these three concepts, you can build a morality toolkit that can help you navigate the known and unknown.

By taking the path of LOM, you can find your morality at any level of society. So much philosophy is the whim of the rich man, who has choices and options. But for those of us who seek the infinite center, LOM gives us the tools to succeed.

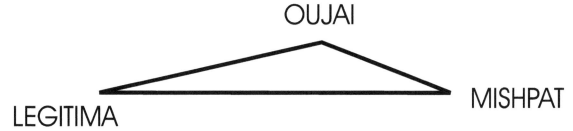

Try these sample problems to see if LOM can help you. If you can find which elements are Legitima, Oujai, and Mishpat, then you may be able to skip preliminary training and dive right in to LOM! You don't have to solve these moral problems. Just see if you can identify the elements.

You live in a country where cannabis is illegal. You have a family member that is suffering from terminal cancer and is experiencing wrenching pain and loss of appetite. You know someone who sells cannabis illegally. What do you do?

You find a gun in a field. Your friends wants to take the gun from you and use it to shoot out the windows of an abandoned house to antagonize the ghosts inside. But you do not believe in ghosts.

You invested in a company that is about to be leveraged via short selling and dismantled. The company makes no product whatsoever, but the name is fun to say and you enjoy shouting it out at every opportunity.

How did you do? Did you break up the details and actions and classify them as Legitima, Oujai, and Mishpat? Then you're already one of us! LOM comes to you as easily as a master! Did you know you had it in you this whole time? I did.

Since you've mastered the most basic concepts, you're ready to start applying circumstances and decisions to the pyramid. For that, you'll need training. Hey, if it were all innate instinct, this system would just be called Oujai and I'd be writing about something else.

Your instinct, your urge toward spirit and divinity, your Oujai, is only part of it. We live in a world with a history and patterns of control and protection. We live with laws and rules. We live in Legitima. The people around us, and we too, have unwritten norms that guide us. They and we have boundaries we can scarcely describe that we just seem to know. We and they have Mishpat.

You can bring any creed you want to LOM. It replaces no creed. LOM is merely a tool to fill in the gaps between high-minded morals and the world which sorely tests them. And, as we all know, the world exists to test us.

TIRE-CON 2022
REGISTRATION NOW OPEN

March 4-6, 2022
SANDUSKY, OH

SEE THE TRUTH

RAINBOWS ARE DEATH RAYS!

THE EYE IS BOMBARDED

COLOR ISN'T REAL
ISN'T REAL COLOR
REAL COLOR ISN'T

LEARN NEW SIGHT

CIRCLE #101 ON CARD

A CENTURY OF TIRE ADVERTISING
RESERVE YOUR SPOT NOW! Panel tickets are
going fast! Limited space available for:
Wagons To Station Wagons * Steel-Belting:
The Next Layer * Amagax Forms and Tread
Duration * Meeting The Road: What's Next

Circle #100 on card.

Have you ever listened to the wind? Often I can hear whispers in the light swirling breeze, or in gusts against my window. But the wind speaks its own language.

God has sent messages to humans in many ways, and at many times throughout history. It only makes sense that God would use the wind, the very stuff of Heaven, to tell us more about Him. And when God uses the wind, it takes its mightiest form—the tornado!

God has been writing on the Earth with tornadoes, and it's time you learned to read what He has to say! We have been sent hidden messages, transmitted over at least five thousand years in a whirl of air, dirt, and debris. All this time, we have been thoughtlessly repairing what we thought was damage and getting on with our mortal lives. We have been erasing God's message!

By utilizing historical weather data to connect the touchdowns of tornadoes and using their "destructive" paths as guides, we can see the actual language of God written upon the earth. What appears to the ignorant as random paths of destruction are in fact deliberate lines of creation. And you can learn this language! We've already lost so much of it, sadly. The only usable tornado data started being kept in 1950, so we can only know God's recent thoughts.

Many will joke about places like Moore, OK, obliterated by majestic tornadoes multiple times in recent history. *Who would want to live there? God seems to have it in for that place.* Hogwash! God is writing his message on Moore and many places like it! These places are holy.

Angels are dangerous beings too, and they are another method of conveying God's message on Earth. But God is sending a different message now. Otherwise he would send angels. God is sending knowledge to those who would discover his medium and learn to understand it.

Below is the panhandle of Oklahoma. These are the connected paths of every tornado for the last seventy years. Separated by EF intensity, patterns emerge.

MICHAEL LOUM

wants to show you the writing of God.

#109 on card

God's writing upon the Oklahoma panhandle, 1950-present.

The script is not only written in space, it is written in time. One stroke is from one decade, the next from another. When will God's script be complete? We cannot know for sure. But consider—there has never been an EF5 tornado in the Oklahoma Panhandle. Is God saving his most emphatic writing for later? Is this a less important passage in the novel he is writing upon the land?

That's correct—I said novel. God is writing a fictional narrative on Earth. It's the story of Slaine Carpenter, survivor of a zombie apocalypse. He survived by eating his own brain to save it. Removing his brain didn't hurt him, because he's a zombie. And zombies don't actually digest anything, so he keeps his brain safe in his stomach. And so when the humans attack him, they're always shooting and hacking his head, but his brain's not there! They don't know *what* to do!

The humans are led by Liberál Satanico, the President of the European Union. They want to wipe out the zombies, and especially their leader, Slaine Carpenter. The EUers want to complete their tyrannical takeover of the world of the living by extending their lives with socialized medicine and vegan diets. They believe that this world is all there is, but the zombies know better!

God's writing upon eastern Wyoming, 1950-present.

I have a good sense of the plot of what I believe to be the sixteenth novel in the series. It's called *THE UNVEGANING*. Given the density of the writing I have thus far translated and the amount of plot revealed, I believe this series will end with the twentieth book and the extinction of all life on Earth.

God is presenting humans with a final message, couched in a series of high-energy, action-packed books. If you don't start reading now, you'll never finish in time. You will definitely not care about God's novels when you're running from brain-eating zombies. And they're going to be the fast kind.

Eastern Wyoming's tornado activity is a thrilling scene where the zombies infiltrate a soybean processing plant in Brussels and taint the tofu with meat. The zombies take little bites of each other, chew them until they're a fine paste, and spit the bites into the mixing vats. The EUers don't become zombies, but their lives are drastically shortened by the meat protein. They won't stay in their earthly paradise as long as they'd hoped!

West Texas is much more difficult to read. Seventy years of scribbling on this obviously holy land has locked away many important details about the fate of Pope Bishop and his zombie cardinals after they fly into the Ukraine to steal massive amounts of gluten to reintroduce into the EUers' breads and crackers. It's possible the EUers have developed a zombie cure, or they may be using microwave cannons to cure the flesh of the zombies, turning them into slow-moving jerky.

If we do not solve these textual problems, we will fall behind in critical events in God's novels. When we die and are challenged at the gates of Heaven, those who cannot offer detailed, specific praise of His work will be cast into the Hell of critics and fools! And woe be unto those that dare to offer constructive criticism! Do you dare to offer advice to God? Do not misuse this knowledge by letting it be a tool of your mortal ego!

God's writing upon West Texas is, admittedly, a little opaque. More study is needed to work out the plot!

As you read this, my team at the Tornadic Narrative Project are poring over weather maps, looking for the narrative beat that signals the end of the series and the original world God made. Will we return in God's new world, recast as a zombie or an EUer? Will knowledge of God's plot for what may be His next creation help you get a speaking role in the live-action version, so to speak? Perhaps.

It's all here, written on the land with God's own finger. Wherever you are right now, God has written something near you. Can you feel His power, the thrill of His holy narrative? You will!

Reprinting *TIRE June 2000* shook the trees of my life hard enough to dislodge some oddities hiding way over my head all these years. That first year after I drew the drawing, a few dedicated weirdos tried very hard to get close to me and the drawing itself. I dimly recall some contentious talk between either of my parents and someone at our front door occasionally during that time. But they kept it away from me until I got a little older.

This next section is a zine from 1979 that I found in a scrapbook. I'd started scanning all the old family pictures, and that necessitated an organization of all the family ephemera. And here it was—the earliest extant Jitting zine.

BETWEEN THE LINES is a classic of the stream of consciousness bang it out on a typewriter genre. You had to be a very determined soul to try zine distro in the late 70s/early 80s. Photocopies weren't cheap yet and the only place you could advertise them was in other zines, or the want ads in *TIRE*.

There are earlier issues, but I haven't seen them. But I'd bet real money that Whitney has the earlier issues. You'll see why.

The author's name is lost to history, though I assume a search of the court records in Prowers or Baca Counties, Colorado might yield it. I'm not that keen to dox the guy all these years later, even though he did it to me. In fact, I have a bit of sympathy for him now.

THE JIT

found this in a scrapbook and wants to share.

#166 on card

He was exactly the sort of person I hoped to defuse by putting a high-res scan of the drawing into the world. For many of those pestering me, it appeared to be enough. They just wanted a good look at the picture. Fair enough.

This zine appears to have changed titles multiple times. But, when it was primarily about me, it was called *BETWEEN THE LINES*. Which is funny, because that's the title of a parking industry magazine now. And they had a guy interview me about parking while asking sneaky JIT-related questions along the way. Even if that is somehow the same guy, he's infinitely less a pest than Whitney is. I can't be bothered to get paranoid about a long game that low-key.

When I ask my mother about this stuff now, she just dismisses it with a wave of her hand and says she doesn't remember that stuff anymore. She's not sure why I want to revisit any of it, now that the Jitters don't invade my life the way they used to. The drawing made being my parents a lot harder than it had to be, so I see her point of view. But, if it wasn't that, it would have been something else. I was accused of being the actual Anti-Christ as a baby (a story told in *TIRE June 2000*), so it was always going to be something.

BETWEEN THE LINES

7th

A MAGAZINE IN PURSUIT OF THE SEVENTH TRUTH

Another winter has passed, and here you are, still reading BETWEEN THE LINES. And for that, I am gratefu -ful. Important work is being done on the drawing, work that demands attention. Your continued support of this magazine guarantees that the world will soon know the full truth of THE GOD OF THE KING.

The portal to the SEVENTH TRUTH was opened by a child, nine year old John Ira Thomas of Lamar, CO. This is as sure a sign that we have depleted the SIXTH TRUTH, provided in a tea towel stain by Mrs. Margaret Illoyne of Thor, MN, as can be granted to us. We must not tarry in catching the new truth train lest we be left at the station with a receipt for eternal life and our baggage at our feet.

Much work is being done on the meaning of the text of the SEVENTH TRUTH--"The God of the King is going into the lions body." But it is important to divine what we can from the picture of the picture. The shapes may appear primitive, but they correspond in form to footwork patterns from at least two of the prominent secret societies in the U.S. (United States (of being!)) today. The most striking match is to the Initiation (First Epoch), plate 22 in the Ritual of the International Order of Jobs Daughters, seen on the next page.

The path of the Pilgrims (initiates) takes them south, then north of the altar, slipping between the Fourth and Fifth Messengers. This path is of interest to us because the Fourth Messenger completes the story of Job to the initiates. The Fifth Messenger then begins to impart the meaning of the story.

This is your path, too. The drawing is drawn, and now we must determine its meaning. But, back to the floorwork pattern.

After moving between the Fourth and Fifth Messengers, the Pilgrims move slightly further north of the altar and form a north-south line in the west. This shape corresponds to the outline of the prone King in his altar in the drawing.

Once in this line, the Pilgrims are told that they are ready for the Second Epoch of the initiation. Even though the Pilgrims have just passed between the Fourth and Fifth Messengers, they hear from the Third Messenger at this point. Job is still suffering. But orders like these always seem to put the cart before the horse.

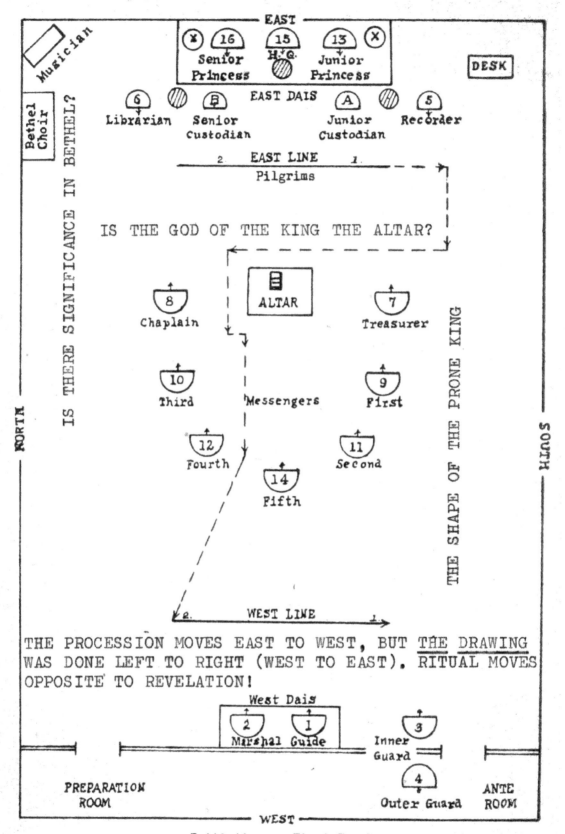

IS THERE SIGNIFICANCE IN BETHEL?

IS THE GOD OF THE KING THE ALTAR?

THE SHAPE OF THE PRONE KING

THE PROCESSION MOVES EAST TO WEST, BUT THE DRAWING
WAS DONE LEFT TO RIGHT (WEST TO EAST). RITUAL MOVES
OPPOSITE TO REVELATION!

Initiation. First Epoch.
Plate 22. WHAT ARE THE DAUGHTERS OF JOB KEEPING FROM US?
FLOOR PLAN

You can call it a coincidence, but the "o" in "Job's Daughters stands for "Order being our first law." As an old DeMolay, I can tell you that any society with a ritual featuring <u>twenty-nine</u> plates of footwork pattern isn't making it up as they go along! This is here for a reason. And I submit that the reason is:

THE DRAWING HAS BEEN WAITING TO BE DRAWN.

Its contours are glimpsed in American rituals of fraternity and sorority. And now that the drawing exists, it must be shared with the world! But there is a problem with that. The secrets have guardians that do not want this special child and his drawing to become public knowledge. We do not know as yet if it is because they wish to share the drawing in their own way, or if they mean to keep this knowledge for themselves. Did they use ritual and magick to breed a child to be the vessel? How long is their spiritual game?

Efforts to directly access the drawing have been met with failure. The parents laugh when told of the significance of <u>the drawing</u>, seemingly oblivious to the glaringly obvious. All we have is a photo taken at some distance with a lucky camera shot over the shoulder of the mother. A second picture was attempted, but it was clear that I was not a television repairman at that point. So I was escorted out.

Other drawings by the child (I do not use his name out of respect for his privacy) have proven to be less than inspiring. A large drawing of a hockey game for National Physical Education Week has some promise, but more study is needed. The path of the puck in the picture seems very deliberate, and indeed may compare to the ritual footwork of the Knights Templar of Illinois. More on that another time.

RESPONSE TO W. TURNER--I have received another missive from Mr. Turner, postmarked North Pole, Colorado in an apparent attempt at anonymity. He writes (in part, because his letters would require publishing an entire other magazine to print in full): "I have received another disappointing issue of BETWEEN THE LINES (neé THROWING ON THE TOWEL). How can you pursue a material object like a fool for so long? You got the tea towel and got no more truth out of the physical object than if you'd soiled your own towel and declared it to be the Fourth Book of the Law! (cont.)

(cont.) The secret of divination is not to chase the detritus produced when the spiritual world emerges, however briefly, in the material world...(B)ecoming that spiritual entity should be the goal? Why wait for knowledge to be granted? Become that which knows! I await your response in the next issue, since I appear to represent around 10% of your subscribers and 100% of your correspondents...."

It is my sincerest wish that there is a Hell, because I want with all my heart for W. Turner and all his elves to go there. Mr. Turner believes he has a captive audience in me. In reality, Mr. Turner, you are my prisoner. Who else would have you? I give you a few lines in my magazine, and you give me a proven audience and the pride of looking like a sane man by comparison. You could quit sending me letters via reindeer, or whatever you think youre doing by sending letters from Santas Workshop, but that would be quitting. And you wouldnt want to be known as the person who lost an argument with a man you called "a person so lost he can hardly be said to have a soul at all." So keep those letters coming.

It is my hope that one day the world can be brought closer together with our words, shared across the world instantly. We can become one great hive mind, sharing our thoughts together in a great project for the improvement of humankind. Once we can share our true selves together, I believe peace will reign over the Earth.

OTHER BUSINESS--Subscriptions are going up again. Wisdom has to cost us something! Subscriptions are now eight (8) stamps, up from six. Please be sure to send $.15 stamps. Im looking at you, Mr. Turner. Remember: you wont know what Im saying about you if you dont subscribe.

TIRE WATCH--TIRE Magazine will be publishing a letter I submitted on the drawing in response to some absolute twaddle they published in their July 1979 issue. The study of the drawing has barely begun and the vultures are already circling my work. I WILL NEVER SELL OUT.

CORRESPONDENCE--Iknow Mr. Turner has my address, but just in case anyone else wants it. BETWEEN THE LINES, Box 1935, Campo, CO 81029. Subscriptions to same.

the God of the King ———⟶ *The Lion's Body*

Mr & Mrs Thomas...

I ask once again that you
read my magazine and
try to understand the value
of your child and his drawing.
If you let me make a copy of
his drawing, I will be more than
happy to leave you alone.
These are truths within this
drawing that can benefit all
mankind! Better yet, if I
could have the original drawing.
Here are the stamps sufficient to
mail the drawing to me, as you have
seen fit to have a restraining order
against me. Please consider this

— Jackson

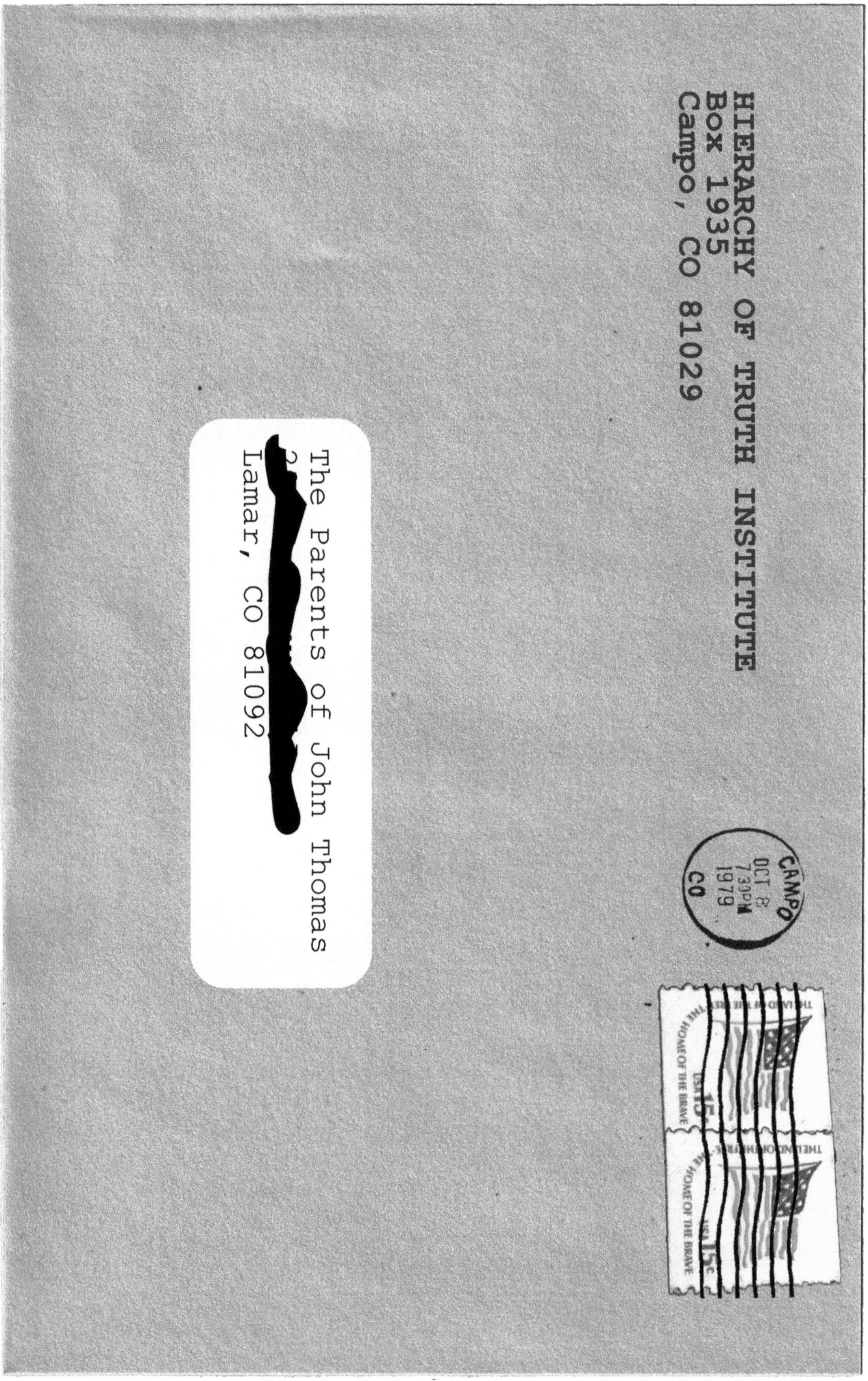

HIERARCHY OF TRUTH INSTITUTE
Box 1935
Campo, CO 81029

The Parents of John Thomas

Lamar, CO 81092

CAMPO
OCT 8
7 30 PM
1979
CO

DRINK LIKE A CAVEMAN

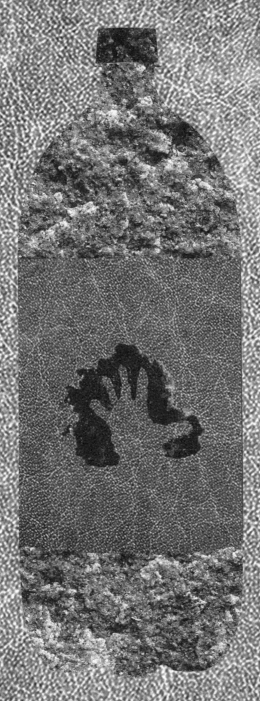

#228 ON CARD

PETRIFIED WATER

I went along with Maddalena to the supermarket the other day, nestled in a carriage like always. Sometimes people will make coo-coo noises and stick their heads in to look for a baby. Finding none, it's an even split between people who are charmed and people who are somehow enraged. I mind my own business in the pram while in the supermarket, but I have personally seen people stick the serving spoon at the salad bar in their mouth.

People make assumptions about dogs. They assume we're dirty, unworthy of presence in sacred human places. They think that about other humans too. Do we kick you out of dog parks, even when you run with your arms dangling saying insane crap like "I feel so free!"

We do not care about your freedom. We work on spells that give you diarrhea when you wear white pants. But Maddalena tells me I'm a good boy, and I can at least aspire to that.

MUGGINS

is a pup with a passion for the way of Wicca.

#131 on card

Just remember that when you stick your head in a baby carriage, it's not on us if you're disappointed. They're your expectations, not our reality. We are not here to be what you want us to be.—*Muggins*

Salutations and greetings, it is I, the one Christians blame for everything wrong with the world. If Eden was so perfect, why was eating fiber a sin? I carry this prejudice everywhere I am carried. I go out with Lars under me and suddenly I get why Middle Eastern people hate *HOMELAND* so much. When all the villains look like you, it's hard not to take it personally when people call the cops.

I am a bull snake. I cannot unlock my jaw and swallow your child. I have no paradise-wrecking produce to distribute. I participate in spells to bring good harvest, and occasionally I move around on an altar of woman for Satanists on Sundays. Lars makes a few bucks and I get a live mouse.

Oh, if you're a mouse, go ahead and be very afraid of me. That's fair. I will eat you.

So think about your fears. I can't wreck paradise, because, well, look around. Your fears can define you and probably make you kinda racist.—*Sidney*

SIDNEY

sssays the answersss are sssimple.

#132 on card

I completely hear where Sidney is coming from this month. Mice are jerks, delicious little jerks. Fight the power, Sidney!

I'm reliably informed that people fear black cats, especially those belonging to Wiccans. This is fine. Anything that keeps people away from me can keep right on, as far as I'm concerned.

There is value in humans' fears. A frightened human will not pet you or confront you when you puke in their shoe. Fear is great. Fear is the foolkiller. Fear is the key, I submit, to world peace.

Who's to say I can't turn into a monster that rends flesh and bone, or turn you into a mouse? Best not to eff around and find out. Sylvain talks about Scooby-Doo when I frighten some fool who says ridiculous things like "puss-puss" to me, but he's high a lot of the time. So there's no telling what that means.

NOODLES

knows you know what he means.

#133 on card

Take that message or take nothing, far as I care. Don't be afraid of the snake, but be very afraid of me. Shoo!—*Noodles*

Let's talk about making time for yourself. As a part of the wondrous cycle of life, you have a lot of responsibilities. You have to remember to rest your active mind and not burn out.

HAMILTON

won't hog all the wisdom of Mother Earth.

#134 on card

It's important that you keep Gaia's priorities utmost in your mind, even in the face of climate change, a continent worth of plastic roaming the oceans and choking out fish, all the calamities that might make you think your part isn't significant. I'm here to tell you that you are an important part of this. You must keep your head high, prioritize nature, and especially, and I can't stress this enough, maintain your commitment to veganism.

I'm not just talking to Selena. I could be talking to anybody. But I've been thinking about this a lot lately because Selena seems dispirited that the rituals and the political action don't seem to be stemming the tide just yet. Also because the first thing former vegans reach for is bacon when they backslide.

I'm serious. Let's get some action on climate change! I might get eaten! Think of the pigs!—*Hamilton*

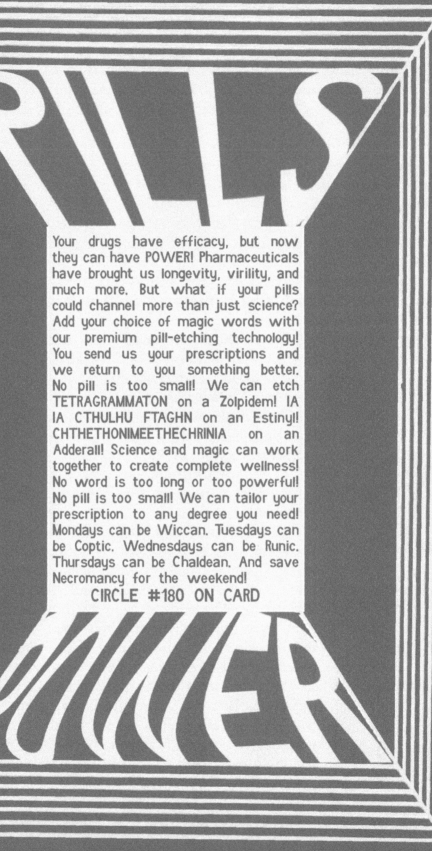

PILLS

Your drugs have efficacy, but now they can have POWER! Pharmaceuticals have brought us longevity, virility, and much more. But what if your pills could channel more than just science? Add your choice of magic words with our premium pill-etching technology! You send us your prescriptions and we return to you something better. No pill is too small! We can etch TETRAGRAMMATON on a Zolpidem! IA IA CTHULHU FTAGHN on an Estinyl! CHTHETHONIMEETHECHRINIA on an Adderall! Science and magic can work together to create complete wellness! No word is too long or too powerful! No pill is too small! We can tailor your prescription to any degree you need! Mondays can be Wiccan. Tuesdays can be Coptic. Wednesdays can be Runic. Thursdays can be Chaldean. And save Necromancy for the weekend!

CIRCLE #180 ON CARD

POWER

Medical science has hit a blind alley. How long have promised cures been delayed? Cancer? Alzheimer's? Autism? The common cold? Where has Medicine gone wrong?

It's nobody's fault. Doctors were on a roll from the germ theory of disease until the 20th Century. People stopped dying from having a cut on their hand. Surgery stopped being a literal race against heart failure.

But we made a wrong turn along the way. In trying to see the future of medicine, we chose a track that led us to breakthroughs that weren't all that helpful compared to the elimination of polio. Again, this is nobody's fault.

Have you read a historical medical treatise? The Greeks thought gynecology was a question of how much bird poop you put into the vagina. And don't get me started about how long doctors thought we were just too full of blood to be healthy. There have been some blind alleys on the way to curing hepatitis C. And we're currently in another one.

Rd. Hod QUERREY

can admit when science is wrong.

#155 on card

Sure, there have been some advances. Boners once again run in great herds not seen since pre-processed food times. We got multiple COVID-19 vaccines along with malaria and AIDS discoveries bound up in that. But we found the boners while looking for a heart drug to replace the old heart drug that went generic. And we got COVID-19 right because we were all going to die. Getting our shit together in a pandemic *proves* we're on the wrong track.

We at the Pivot Institute have identified the year where it all started to go wrong, and have jettisoned all medical research from that time forward. This is not a thought experiment. We've tossed the Viagra and the oxycodone and are trying again. We keep the successes of the succeeding 90 years, but use them as guiding lights.

We've abandoned the blind alley from 1931 onward and have gone back to re-ask key questions that no doctor today would dream to address. Does mental derangement have a combination of spiritual and dental causes? Did we abandon guano-based gynecological treatments too soon? Are needle injection points too narrow? Does the endocrine system present the opportunity for eternal life? How many testicles do we need? Our redoctors are on the case!

These are crucial questions that must be answered. We can laugh and pretend that we know these things, but we don't. Not for sure. The Greeks would have been surprised to find that the brain is not merely an organ for cooling the blood. You probably didn't know hep C had been defeated. Assumptions keep us from future knowledge. We're not here to place leeches. We're here to move forward, in the right direction this time. Consult a redoctor today!

There is an untapped source of Karma in the world, the moral value applied to the omission of evil. You and I collect this whenever we don't harm someone. We do it all day long. It's not a lot of moral value, but it's not nothing. And when things have value, the financial services sector eventually comes calling.

In 2015, the first vessels were constructed, according to exacting standards that have become the backbone of the token market. These vessels are defined as individuals with enough moral agency for their inaction to have value. Bugs, birds, and animals are stored with them to provide the opportunity for harm. But since the vessels do nothing, every minute a bug remains unsquashed creates value. Once you unlock the door to moral agency for one undone act, the whole spectrum of undone acts becomes available to the vessel!

Our vessels are unique individuals, tied to code protected by blockchain technology. If you tie together enough vessels that do not lie, cheat, steal, murder, eat meat, or think even one impure thought, you've generated something of value. Bundle them together and you have moral tokens that can help clinch your afterlife status! By leveraging the simple and valuable morality of inaction, you can have it all!

A man in South Carolina collected enough tokens in two years to start a second family in a bunker and keep them there for their entire lives. A fourteen-year-old in Michigan can murder three people and face God with a pure heart. Combines are already forming to see if enough tokens can be generated to wipe the slate clean for state-level actions.

Doesn't this legalize murder, you ask? No, it merely legitimizes it. These tokens will not help you with legal complications, only moral and spiritual ones. There's already a token to get you out of legal trouble—it's called money.

Doesn't this create a murder free-for-all? You ask a lot of questions, and I like that about you! The more tokens you hold, the more moral import you possess. Those without tokens are only morally valuable to the extent of their earthly actions and deeds, and plenty of people already have enough tokens to kill someone like that.

But there is no agreed value to murdering someone who has tokens in their spiritual portfolio. So it's important you get started with your vessels, to set them up and start collecting tokens from their morality of inaction. Someone might be collecting enough tokens to get away with killing you. Most murder victims are killed by someone they know.

Koeller SANDOVAL

sees the value in doing nothing.

#188 on card

Now that tokens are so valuable, a secondary market of spiritual microtransactions has sprung up. Arranged correctly, special financial instruments can be devised that let you get a lot of bang for your buck. A small percentage of a token can be used to start a chain of events that leads to a death without intending that death in the commission of the act—say, the misplacing of an EpiPen, or a careless word about someone's fidelity to an easily agitated spouse.

There are a multitude of token types—Karma tokens, Kantian tokens, Utilitarian tokens, Egoism tokens. The sky's the limit! Create your own token type and carve your own path in the moral inaction markets!

You can even find value in unused papal indulgences. A written record of a warrior of the Crusades that was submitted to Pope Urban but never processed went for tokens totaling one hundred and thirty acts of adultery back in 2018. An unopened letter of forgiveness to an unfaithful spouse found in a trunk dating back to the eighteenth century went for a lifetime pass on eating veal.

The ground floor on this is long gone, but that doesn't mean you shouldn't dive right in! The only cost to inaction is not doing it! You can't afford not to!

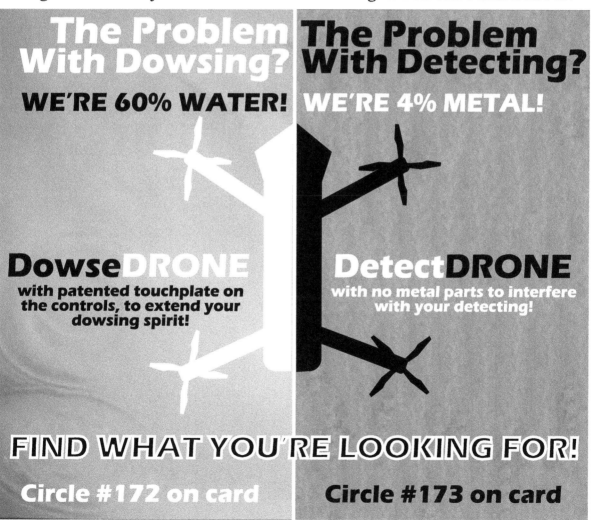

FROM YOUR LIPS TO ONLY GOD'S EARS

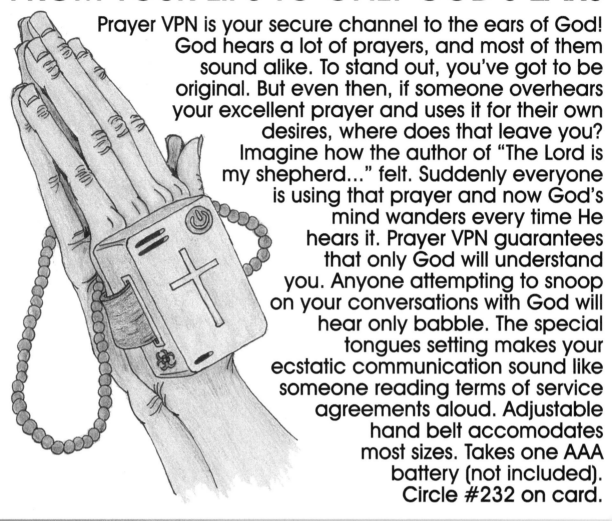

Prayer VPN is your secure channel to the ears of God! God hears a lot of prayers, and most of them sound alike. To stand out, you've got to be original. But even then, if someone overhears your excellent prayer and uses it for their own desires, where does that leave you? Imagine how the author of "The Lord is my shepherd..." felt. Suddenly everyone is using that prayer and now God's mind wanders every time He hears it. Prayer VPN guarantees that only God will understand you. Anyone attempting to snoop on your conversations with God will hear only babble. The special tongues setting makes your ecstatic communication sound like someone reading terms of service agreements aloud. Adjustable hand belt accomodates most sizes. Takes one AAA battery (not included). Circle #232 on card.

CRYSTAL DENTAL APPLIANCES

We can place crystal power where you need it most—in your mouth! Sodalite bridges can grind hard seeds while soothing your spirit and reducing your EM spectrum exposure. An amethyst crown will protect you from nightmares and tartar. Onyx braces will deflect hurtful criticism while guiding your teeth to true straightness. A malachite retainer will reduce menstrual cramps while helping you retain the shape of your bite. Our new subperiosteal implants let you swap out crowns for maximum crystal power. Need a quick shift from honesty to willpower? Just use our patent-pending crown wrench to unscrew your amazonite crown and slip on a citrine one. It's so easy! Don't have any teeth left? Try our line of crystal dentures! You can slot in every major crystal with gum to spare to double or triple up on your favorites! Or you can go one crystal for the top and another for the bottom. Think of your communication skills with a complete set of turquoise teeth! Don't be fooled by dentists that glue tiny cosmetic crystals on existing teeth—Crystal Dentistry's benefits only come to those who commit to the whole tooth! Circle #291 on card.

FILLINGS, BRACES, CROWNS

YOU ARE THE INFINITE OR ANGE

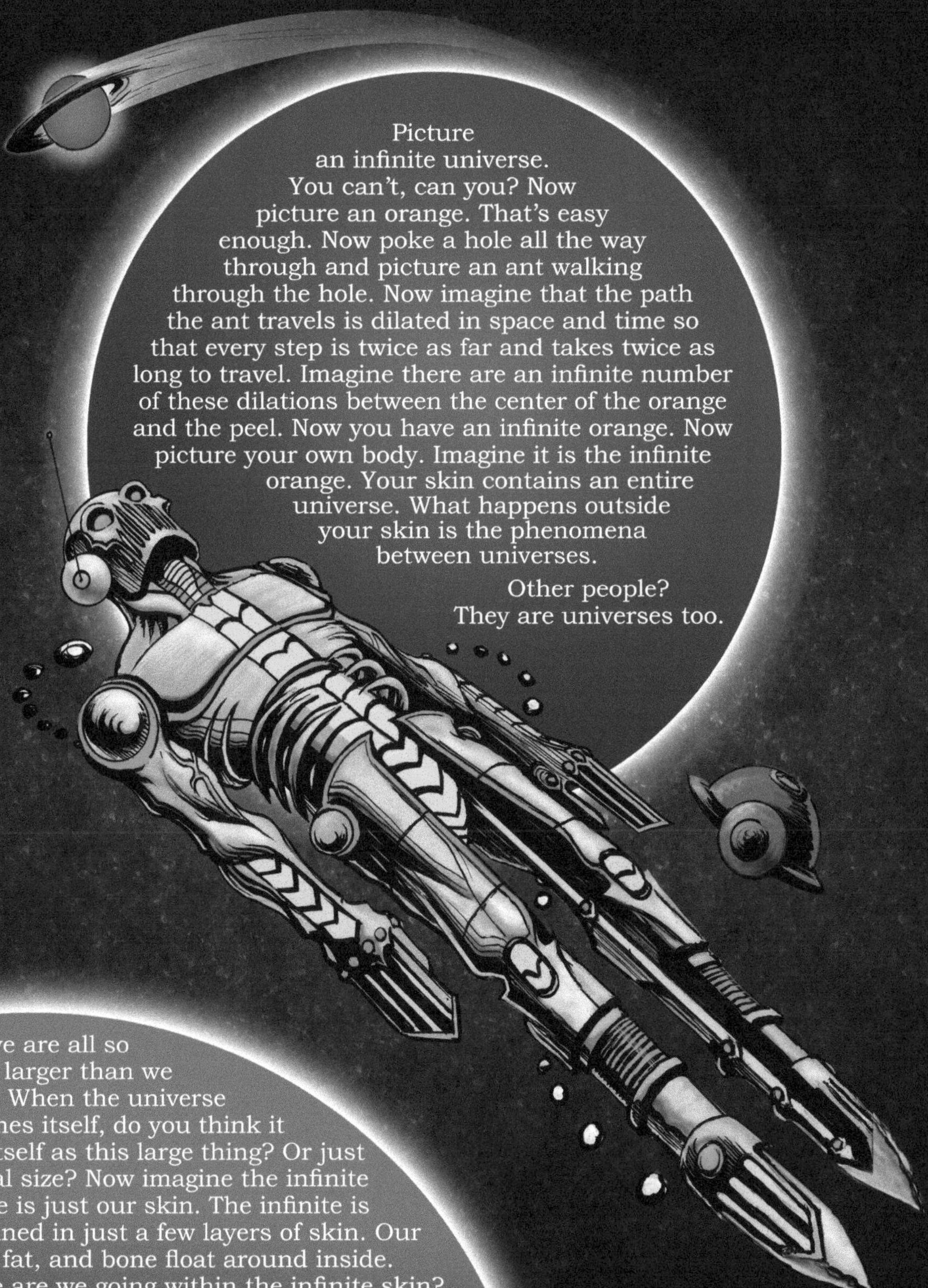

Picture
an infinite universe.
You can't, can you? Now
picture an orange. That's easy
enough. Now poke a hole all the way
through and picture an ant walking
through the hole. Now imagine that the path
the ant travels is dilated in space and time so
that every step is twice as far and takes twice as
long to travel. Imagine there are an infinite number
of these dilations between the center of the orange
and the peel. Now you have an infinite orange. Now
picture your own body. Imagine it is the infinite
orange. Your skin contains an entire
universe. What happens outside
your skin is the phenomena
between universes.

Other people?
They are universes too.

And we are all so
much larger than we
think. When the universe
imagines itself, do you think it
sees itself as this large thing? Or just
normal size? Now imagine the infinite
orange is just our skin. The infinite is
contained in just a few layers of skin. Our
meat, fat, and bone float around inside.
Where are we going within the infinite skin?
Do you want to float aimlessly? Do you want
your universe to have no meaning? Or do you
want to find your bodyship and explore?
Circle #177 on card.

ASTROLOGY IS YESTERDAY'S FUTURE!

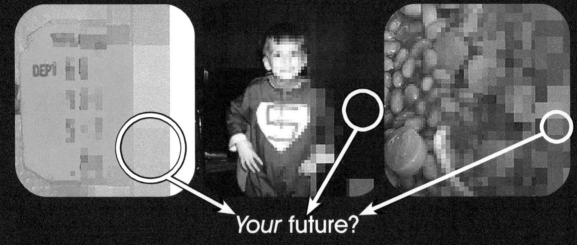

Your future?

The new future is PIXELGNOSIS. The arrangement of stars has not proven to be the predictor of events that we'd all hoped. It's fine. We all make mistakes. The ancients had no idea that it would be the arrangement of pixels on the Internet that would chart all our fates. Learn to spot the special pixels! See the special distances to be measured between them! Know what our pixelgnostics already know—the future! Circle #266 on card.

WE ENDED THE COLD WAR

What should we end next? Our prayer circle is looking for the next big challenge! Earthly preferences dilute our power, so you tell us what's up! Should we end flag burning? Sharia law? Democrat voting? Let us know! Circle #294 on card.

JOIN US AT NICAEA! SEPTEMBER 17-19 2021

It's time for a new Bible, and you can get in on the ground floor! Bring your new books of the Bible to Nicaea, KY and we'll work out a new Bible the way the Church has done it for centuries! Nothing is apocryphal until we say it is! All testimonies welcome! Who wouldn't want to see a Book of Becky, or a Book of Skyler, or a Book of [YOUR NAME HERE]? For a modest fee, your testament can receive special consideration from our council! Because, let's be honest—the council is just going to skim a lot of them. But by showing your earnestness with a love offering, you can give your words the extra lift they need to reach God's ears! Writing and epiphany workshops still have a few openings left! Campground packages also available (no RV hookups). Act now to secure your place in religious history! Don't open the next testament with regrets! Circle #263 on card.

YOUR HAIR IS YOUR DESTINY!

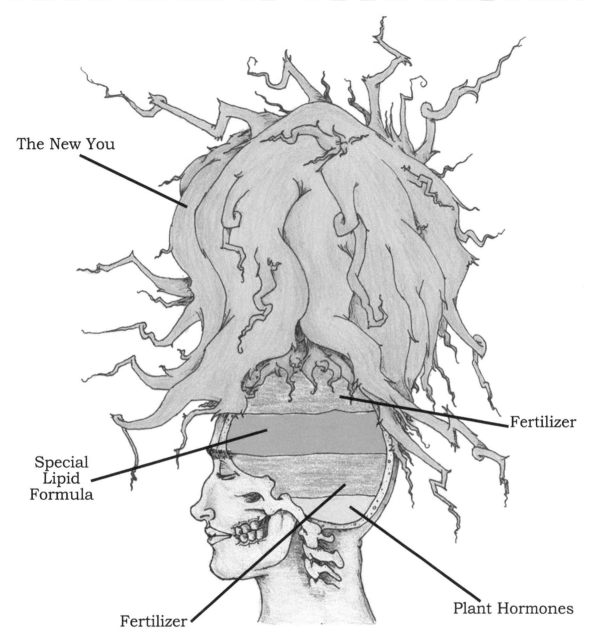

The New You

Fertilizer

Special Lipid Formula

Fertilizer

Plant Hormones

The sentience of our hair has been held back by our tiny life spans! Make a post-life plan that helps bring about the next stage of human evolution! With a simple preprinted codicil to your will or power of attorney, you can arrange for your estate to prepare you for the awakening of your hair! Postmortem, our team will empty your head and replace the contents with our patented four layer hair-growing formula. Your skin will glow, and you'll become a perfect dewy monument to yourself! Your hair will continue to grow and look silky and lustrous for the moment it achieves sentience. Will it be you? Of course! It's your hair, after all! Just send for our easy to fill out codicil, enter the key details, and drop it into the prepaid return envelope! We'll take care of the rest! The first hair to awaken will have a head start on the rest! Don't delay! **Circle #235 on card.**

The age of fun little pamphlets that get to their insane point and bail is a thing of the past. The great pamphlets were like jazz for crazy people. They were exactly as long as they needed to be. Nowadays, everyone wants to write a book. Problem is, these people still have exactly the same amount of ideas.—JIT

91 TO GO: MY JOURNEY TO 178 by Rich Gilortny $19.95

Rich has a plan to extend his life by a very specific number of years. It's a lot of exercise and learning not to poop anymore. In his desperate attempt to drag his pamphlet of mostly horrible advice across the 100-page mark, he drops the news that there will be a total polar shift in 87 years. He plans to grow gills by this point to make it through the last four years of his extended existence. He has no actual plan for growing the gills, so I guess that's the sequel.

ASTROLOGY ON THE CRAPPER by Dorna Istlewine $19.95

Earth's millionth book on Astrology starts with a nugget I can get behind. When you're siting on the toilet, cosmic wisdom comes to you more easily. It reminds me of a line from *PROMETHEUS BOUND* about Poseidon's chariot—seated in a chair over the rushing waves. The cover and title make me think this thing is sold at truckstops next to fart spray. Anyways, dangling your sensitive parts over water gives you a deeper connection to the Earth and the stars will tell you more because...they feel sorry you have dangly parts? Honestly, I fell asleep under this one.

PASSWORDS FOR HAPPINESS by Neil Portfjorder $19.95

Nothing tips your hand on a deterministic worldview like suggesting there are literal passwords to open up states of consciousness. Billy Batson does it, why can't you? Seriously, though, if Captain Marvel has the wisdom of Solomon, why does he ever let himself revert to someone only smart enough to sell newspapers? Oh, God is your IT Department, find your protocol to handshake with the divine... oh, and here daemons are good things.

WE HAVE FAILED CANCER by Horst Villanuelle $19.95

Here's a cheery notion. Cancer is our bodies' attempt to complete first-generation evolutionary improvements. But when cancer kills us, it's because we have failed to prepare ourselves for these evolutionary improvements. So when cancer kills you, it's because you failed cancer. Meet the asshole who's on cancer's side. His name's Horst, and he wants twenty bucks.

YOUR BRAIN IS THE BARRIER by Aurine Ourht $19.95

Drugs are bad for your brain, and Aurine means all of them. Aspirin is bad for your brain, even. So, instead of fretting about whether drugs can cross the blood/brain barrier, you can learn to toughen up the old bean to resist all drugs. You may ask why not just abstain from drugs instead of engaging in some frankly intense brain training? Because, in a fun twist, drugs are great for the rest of the body! And she means all of them. Even heroin is great for the body, as long as you clench your brain and keep it out of there. Bonus points for the twist ending.

Included in the tapes from the red case were letters received in response to the June 2000 issue. Six were from Whitney, and you can guess what those were about. So let's give voice to some pissed-off subscribers and slighted charlatans instead, shall we?—JIT

You're Gonna Have To Finish Yourself Off, Guy.

Am I really going to round out my subscription reading about steel-belted radials instead of steeling my soul for astral travel? I'M SO CLOSE YOU CAN'T STOP NOW!—*P. Dochert, St. Agar, MN*

Read This One 21 Years Too Late. Sorry!

If you are ending publication of the true *TIRE*, only to let the false *TIRE* take its place, I propose an alternative. The new old *TIRE* should be its own magazine. The current *TIRE* should continue to be published with blank pages, to signify the loss of such an important periodical. And, since it would be a waste to publish blank pages, you could print the enclosed manuscript. Just so it doesn't look odd on the newsstand. I await your confirmation of this plan and your eternal gratitude for boosting your circulation many times while enlightening the world.—*C. Washler, Quenqueri, ME*

I Only Got A Scan Of The Ten, So Nah.

I WAS TWELVE ISSUES AWAY FROM A COMPLETE COLLECTION OF *TIRE* AND YOU BURNED THEM ALL? THIS IS AN OUTRAGE! ENCLOSED IS TEN DOLLARS. PLEASE AT LEAST SEND ME THE ASHES OF THE 1972 ISSUES SO THAT I CAN HAVE A COMPLETE COLLECTION IN SPIRIT!—*Q. Cossley, Pod, MT*

Read This One 21 Years Too Late. Shit.

Thank you for your article on my best friend Bacon the Psychic Dog. He wanted me to tell you that you may think you're done with *TIRE*, but *TIRE* isn't done with you. This was in a dream, so you should trust that I understood him good.—*J. Eerdorn, Slapout, OK*

If You'd Called It "Bullshit" I'd Say It Right.

It's pronounced sorCELics, you absolute moron. If the rope on the tetherball of knowledge even brushed your pole, you would die of shock at knowing anything of value for once in your life.—*D. Rockley, Plainview, TX*

This Guy Gets It.

Your transformation doesn't fool this seeker. Changing *TIRE* from a magazine openly searching for truth to a "tire and rubber industry" magazine. Oh dear, I guess I better give up looking for knowledge in *TIRE* now! *Wink!* There won't be any astral importance in this article on tire pressure, *Wink!* We are ready for the next stage of *TIRE*'s development. To the clever reader, you won't have changed a bit.—*S. Bellend, Surrey, UK*

A mysterious white man with a bag of apple seeds wandered the American West, dispensing his burden and spreading apple trees throughout the the country.

WAS THAT JESUS?

A mysterious white man in a bear skin told French fur traders in 1728 that they had built Fort Beauharnois on land too low to withstand flooding.

WAS THAT JESUS?

A mysterious white man entered a coffee shop in Nome, Alabama, drank one cup of coffee and left a fifty dollar tip.

WAS THAT JESUS?

Seriously, we're looking for Jesus. We found out the other Jesus was a foreigner, so we have to set about looking for the real Jesus.

THE AMERICAN JESUS INSTITUTE
"making Jesus just like you"
Circle #231 on card

THE BASTINADO METHOD

Earnestine Bastinado's Course of Negative Miracles has stormed three continents with a bold new vision of curses that can work Negative Miracles in your life! Curses and imprecations were once the purview of dead-ender witches, necromancers, and bloody-minded dabblers who all ended up gored on the point of a very broad metaphor when all was said and sacrificed. Laying curses on people revealed the world of magic to be a zero-sum game. And curses uniformly exact a direct cost on the the curser as well as the cursed. But a breakthrough in curse technology has brought us the Negative Miracle! A curse normally laid upon a human or animal can now be cast upon an inanimate object. With no negative effect upon the cursed, the cost upon the caster is negated! And with creative use, the Negative Miracle can be used to draw suppressive forces from your life to affect no one! Imagine a charm cursed to have all the suppressive forces nearby directed to it—just bury it in a nearby lot and watch all the bird shit and stray lightning strikes thump into a metal trinket that doesn't know the difference between pleasure and pain! Watch its credit score tumble to zero as somehow its wife starts sleeping around on it! All the negative forces in your area will focus on the trinket instead of you! That's a Negative Miracle in action! And unlike miracles or other positive spells, you don't have to be spiritually pure to cast a Negative Miracle. In fact, the worse you are, the more powerful the Negative Miracle will be! So don't delay! Start heaping garbage on an old wedding ring or tongue piercing! Make your life better by steering life's cannons of misery away from your position! Circle #213 on card.

FOR CURSES THAT WORK

PUT GOD TO SLEEP

Attention from gods is never a good thing. Gods have opinions, and you're not a god. So, how do you think you'll measure up? Special somnolence runes carved on a crown of St. John's wort will make you just another gray blur in the gods' vast field of vision. The longer an entity stares at it, the sleepier it gets! The one thing gods cannot abide is boredom. Just pop it on whenever you feel noticed by ethereal forces and the crown does the rest! Studies show deity visitations at or near zero to nine decimal points when wearing the crown! Keep your head down and exist!

Circle #242 on card.

BRING THE OCCULT TO YOUR NEIGHBORHOOD!

Want to grow your sect, but aren't sure how your neighbors will react to your teachings? Build a Little Free Temple! Then stock it with a few pamphlets to explain the softer edges of your worldview. Our plans packet includes several basic designs to blend in with the little free libraries in your neighborhood. You build it to your liking, put it up in your yard, and watch your sect grow!

Circle #251 on card.

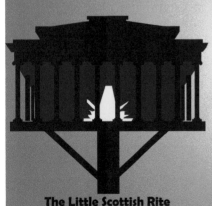

The Little Scottish Rite
Supreme, ancient, and accepted anywhere.

The Little Midsommar
As Harga takes, so Harga also gives.

The Little R'lyeh
Take a book, leave your soul.

Renfield and de la Cruz

The 2022 Harvest Life Almanac is now on sale! Do you serve a master with dark power? There are a lot of natural and supernatural variables to consider as you carry out their infernal plans! You might be able to keep the cycles of the Moon straight in your head, but that's just one tiny part of your job! Birth cycles of relevant insect species, standard to metric conversions for volumes of different creatures' blood, new variations in food technology that alter the taste of potential prey—the smallest detail can mean the difference between grudging acceptance by your master or a gory death in a moment of disappointment over the smallest detail gone wrong. Don't let fate take a hand...or your chance at eternal life! Get the knowledge you need so your master can feed!

Circle #236 on card.

SPECIAL COCKROACH TINCTURES

will make disgusting pests taste like Junior Mints! We will remove all the bugs from your home and put them into your belly! We could try to sell you a book of insect recipes and tell you that frying roaches in curry and ghee will be delicious, but you know better. If they don't taste good in the first place, you're always going to know that you're eating something that tastes terrible. We're here to help! Taste technology has become so advanced that McDonald's can make a pile of sawdust taste like chicken nuggets. Just shake a little of our yummy taste tinctures onto a roach and pop it in your mouth. Once you train your gag reflex to take a hike, you're on the most sustainable food source there is! What do roaches taste like? Anything you want—sizzling cheeseburger, pineapple upside-down cake, any delicious food your heart desires that the Earth will soon be unable to provide! It's time to face facts. The insects are winning the war for dominance over the Earth. We spent all our time thinking we were making the world in God's image. But all we really did was make it into an insect paradise. So we have to do what any apex predator can do—adapt to new prey. Our flavor powders will turn those pests into your new primary food source. Be the lion or shark of the age of Kingdom Insecta! Embrace your new role as predator! Break the bug to belly barrier!

Circle #248 on card.

The City of Dubuque, Iowa is employing car psychics as traffic wardens. "We got a lot of complaints and ticket appeals from people claiming they only parked because of an emergency," says City Traffic Manager Endyne Fossett. "And either you take their word for it and call them on it when they seem to have a lot of emergencies, or you try something new."

Last June, three job postings appeared on the City of Dubuque website. The applicants had to have a good knowledge of parking regulations, and they had to be psychic. "Psychic turned out to be too broad a category," recalls City Councilperson Verna Tomelveny. "It takes too much talent to find a car's driver and divine their thoughts."

What they eventually settled on were psychometrists, a type of psychic who

can read impressions left on objects—specifically, cars. "We're actually reading psychic remnants imprinted on cars by their drivers," says traffic warden Pete Hemmelrai. "People have intense experiences in cars, and the amount of time people spend in them make cars natural psychic sounding boards."

The tickets were reprinted to let the town know what was backing up their violations. Tickets were withheld if the traffic warden sensed an emergency. But fines were multiplied based on intent.

"If I touch a Corolla and I get the vibe of 'I'll just be here a minute,' that's parking with intent, a 2x multiplier," says Hemmelrai. "If I see an expired meter, I'll give the meter a little scan and see if they even touched it."

The town has largely embraced the changes. Traffic warden Moon Fordyce enjoys the little bits of thanks people leave behind. "Sometimes I'll touch a legally parked car by accident and get a clear, deliberate mental note like 'We really appreciate what you do for our community.' And that's great."

Fordyce admits that some of the notes aren't so friendly. "Sometimes the repeat offenders will try to imprint some disgusting image on their car to get a rise out of us. But all we feel is the impotent anger of someone who refuses to understand that if you park at a meter, you pay the meter."

Tickets are about the same as before, but the appeals have dropped considerably. A lawsuit alleging illegal search was tossed out, as the traffic wardens established that people leave their psychic impressions everywhere.

"We don't enter the car," says Hemmelrai. "I don't even look inside. So it's not a search. If we were reading their minds directly, they might have a case there."

"You also get people trying to imprint an emergency on their car," says Fordyce. "But those are easy to see through. Imprinting an emergency on a car in an ADA stall in front of a hardware store is like declaring five-alarm chili an emergency."

The third traffic warden hired quit not long after he started, so an opening has been posted on the City of Dubuque website. He found the job didn't suit him. City Traffic Manager Fossett explains: "Dean, well he was checking meters and he touched a green Chevelle and he sensed a long, loud scream. When the police opened the trunk, they found a dead hitchhiker." Fossett chuckles. "It was funny, too, because they got the search warrant based on the psychometric response. That lawsuit was way off in the end."

This article originally appeared in heavily truncated form in MODERN PSY, *but was also submitted to* TIRE *because of what must be an hilariously outdated mailing list. Since* MP *only used "Dubuque Psychics Driven To Read Car Thoughts Instead Of Honing Their Craft," (which, me-ow, seriously) I felt comfortable printing it in full here. And, since I'm not psychic, the author shall remain unknown. Is that a thing with psychic magazines? They just know who wrote everything?—JIT*

THE FUTURE IS A BOMB
THAT YOU CAN'T SEE COMING!
BUT PROPHESY IS A BOMB TOO!
ARM YOURSELF!

There is a prophesy trigger in your brain! It is a neuron so powerful that it can drown out every other thought in your mind. You can see it in fish. There is a neuron in fish brains that makes them thrash when they're out of the water. That one fish neuron fires, and that's all that is on that fish's mind. You have that neuron too. But it doesn't fire when you're out of the water—it fires when you're out of your depth! Prophesy will fire that neuron! It will blow out every useless thought you have. And in that moment, you will see! But right now, prophesy-wise, your mind is like a baby's—tiny and wrinkle-free.

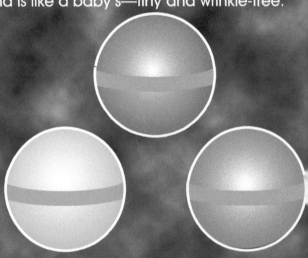

The prophesy neuron cannot be fired by will alone. Like the atomic bomb, it requires another bomb to set it off. It can be risky business to fire your prophesy neuron, which is why it's best done underwater, in your tub. The water will insulate you like the womb, protecting you when the prophesy bomb explodes! You must prepare your mind to be reborn, to flush the toxin that is consensus reality! Common sense is a term for the dead. The important knowledge is far from common, and cannot be sensed by everyone.

That's why you should only use our deity-approved line of prophesy bath bombs to light the fire in your mind! Available in Apocalypse Red Apple, Big Blueberry Marble, and Greenhouse Goddess.

Circle #162 on card

UISPHE CROCODILUS HUMANUS

Our creed began when a humble podiatrist named Emily Volkanoff Keyes accepted the message and transported it to our realm with her dictaphone in 1907. These transcriptions were published as the TESTAMENT OF UISPHE. The Uisphers took every word as completely true and the sect was done by 1938.

Stories like the Canvass of Angels, where God sent angels to prop up the beasts of the world to see which would become human, were dead ends even to the true believers. Other stories seemed more true to them, and they left.

But this gave way to a new creed based on the same text. Gullibilism is believing in the literal meaning of the text (but not really). It is a trancelike state of what psychiatrists call dissonance. We know it to be the spiritual exception to the physics precept that two things cannot occupy the same space at the same time! Think of a pitcher of water. Do they not occupy the same space at the same time? But this, too, failed. And now we know why. Uisphe is meant to be taken literally!

And here's your free revelation—we are not human. The angels got it wrong. The angels chose the wrong animal to become human! It was clearly the crocodile, genetically unchanged since prehistoric times, that should have become human! They didn't realize the tail would become prehensile once crocs learned to walk upright. The true human race has been denied its existence! But we can right this wrong. Send now for more revelations and crocodile assistance packages!

Circle #274 on card.

Sitting here in the last surviving piece of the *TIRE* offices, I feel stories and experiences returning to me. The chair still creaks and leans back too far. I'm worried that if I give it a hit of WD-40, it'll silently dump me on the floor if I shift even a little.

If I close my eyes and work the creaks just right, I can picture myself back in the little house on Corley Street. With twenty years' distance, I can only feel a little of the angst and terror I felt in that month of making the June 2000 issue of *TIRE*.

When I turn the chair to the right I get the WEEERRT squeak—that's where the wall-mounted phone was, the only one in the office. Kids will reel at the thought of nailing your phone to something, but I was a latecomer to cell phones and this was my connection to the outside world. Well, it was my connection to Ruth's office. And pestering her was my only other activity besides writing, sleeping, and staring into space.

It reminds me now of Lucian of Samosata's *MENIPPUS GOES TO HELL*. Menippus, wanting to asked the deceased Tereisias about the meaning of life, conspires with a mysterious priest to visit Hades. The priest covers him in shit, until Menippus looks and smells so bad that nobody will look at him when he passes. Once he is socially deleted, he is able to pass from the land of the living with ease and without dying.

THE JIT

can't believe he used to have that much hair.

#116 on card

I too had disappeared from the world, and entered my own Hell (at least the home of my tormentors). I had no one to ask about much of anything. Ruth had no guidance to offer, except a preface that was mostly legally necessary for her machinations in the Corley empire.

Menippus wanted to ask Tereisias about the meaning of life because he had lived as both man and woman (he pissed off Zeus once). What was my question? Who could I ask? I journeyed to Hell and found it empty. So I tried calling Ruth. But she was always out. Even Tereisias had fled.

After I tried showing up at her office, she assigned me one of the Corley cousins. His job was to shrug at me and eat popsicles. Ruth didn't have to be half as smart as she is to get one over on this crowd, that was for sure.

But I'd learned my lesson. I was on my own in this endeavor. The only thing the June 2000 issue of *TIRE* had to be about was about 120 pages. Failure to do so meant supervision with the same amount of guidance as before. So I told (Endic? Is that a name? Honestly, the kid was a blank slate.) that I knew exactly what I needed to do and didn't need any help.

I didn't see him again until after I burned all the back issues of *TIRE* in a backyard ceremony that I'll call my insomnia purge. He said "Ruth says don't burn stuff." And he left a sticky fire extinguisher. He was much nicer than the firemen were. Firemen are not cool with necessary acts of expiation.

When I turn to the left, I get the VEEENT squeak—that's when I would face the door and decide to trudge back to the Quaker Square Hotel, my home for the month. Ruth put me up in a hotel in Akron that used to be grain silos for Quaker Oats. It's a dorm for the U of Akron now. (Go Zips!)

Living in a hotel does nothing to shake existential dread. It's desert island living. If you know how to make everything out of coconuts, it's fine. If not, you sit and wait for death.

It had been 20-some years since I haunted the Stagecoach Inn in Lamar, Colorado as a little kid. Back then, it was a huge playground to me. The lounge singer in the bar would launch into "Big Bad John" when I'd walk in looking for a Coke.

At Quaker Square, it was different. The staff mostly kept their distance, because they knew the Corleys were paying my tab. That meant I was important and not to be discussed. So of course they assumed the worst.

Living out of a hotel room for a month also puts you apart from the world. About two weeks in one of the staff worked up the nerve to ask me to settle their bet. The big money was on me being an unacknowledged Corley family member who'd fallen on hard times.

I told them I was the guest editor of *TIRE* for one month because the magazine had ruined my life and I was being given a chance to have my say. They had to cancel the pool and give all the money back. They also stopped asking me if I needed anything.

Even in Hell, I was socially deleted. But where do you go when Hell ignores you? Back to the little house on Corley Street

And when I lean back I get the GAWNNNK squeak—and it still makes me want to go burn stuff in the backyard. Because right behind my chair was a wall of neatly arranged back issues of *TIRE*. If you ordered a back issue, some intern would go the wall and fill the order.

At first, I played passive-aggressive games with the wall of *TIRE*. I'd get up suddenly and send the steel and leather chair coasting into the stacks, hoping to damage or dislodge a few. I'd toss a book submitted for review over my shoulder to see if I could at least dent a few. But one day, as I leaned back to ponder something, one issue toppled seemingly on its own and landed on my face.

It would be a better story if I said it was the March '79 issue, the one that started all this. It was October '88, some bullshit cover story about AIDS being a cancerous flaw in the human aura. Was everyone worse in the 80s?

I slapped the issue onto the floor and pulled the whole wall down on top of me. Offense had multiplied upon offense. I spent hours hauling every issue into the backyard and dumping it into a suspiciously clean barrel that probably used to be an astral cannon. Okay, I know it was an astral cannon. They sold those things for TWO HUNDRED DOLLARS in *TIRE* back in the 90s. You sit in the thing and meditate and it was supposed to point your spirit to the astral plane, because apparently your soul is the dim cousin version of yourself. Well, now it was a burn barrel.

There was no shortage of matches around the *TIRE* offices, because New Agers are always burning something. I lit matches and looked for passages through the pile of *TIRE*s that would take the flame close to the bottom. I don't know why I thought this expensive barrel could actually become a cannon, but I really wished that I could have shot a fireball made of *TIRE* into the heavens. When the fire got going, I felt a powerful sense of relief, a first shit in five days toe-stretching kind of relief.

I don't dance. But I danced around that goddamn barrel. Watching them burn, feeling the heat, thrilling to my heart pounding out a warning that I also don't do cardio either...I rode that high right up until a fireman collared me so they could contain my joy with a chemical extinguisher. Magic may be bullshit, but ritual can be magnificent stuff.

Sitting straight and still, the chair makes no noise at all. And I can think clearly. This usually gets me into trouble. I recently spent an evening digging up old proprietary chargers to resurrect phones that hadn't booted up in a decade or more. Finding nothing on any of them, I remembered that 2000 was a pre-cell phone era for me. I'd wasted an entire evening chasing rabbits. Sitting in the old *TIRE* chair seems to bring that out in me.

From there I went to photo albums. At some point, I had bought a disposable camera from the gift shop in the hotel. There were a lot of pictures of my feet dangling in the hotel jacuzzi. Even now this is a tradition when I travel. No matter how long the journey, if I soak my feet when I get there, it's all better. So here are some of those pictures. When I look at them, I can feel the relief of those evenings.

The stretch of time between my receiving the plane ticket to Akron, Ohio and my weeping in front of the guy at the Deli Corner at the Akron-Canton Airport when he asked me if I wanted a pickle spear was a month-long blur. I did want the pickle spear. But instead of saying yes, I dumped a lot of backed-up emotion all over this poor guy.

This makes sense. Airports are liminal spaces. Most people do not have the airport as their final destination. The Deli Corner guy does. But he works there.

For everyone else, it's the door to somewhere else. It's the place that confronts you with the reality that you're going home, or Orlando. I was leaving *TIRE* world and going back to the life *TIRE* had besieged.

I had spent a month creating another iteration of my personal demon. I had been Ruth's weapon, a smart bomb used to destroy only what she wanted destroyed and little else. And now the bay was empty, my payload deployed. I had thought, so clearly and so many times, never again.

But now the chair has found me. The ghosts of the little house on Corley Street live in my house now. But I'm not meant to destroy anything this time.

This trip to Hell will have a purpose, though. I will have my answer. I am leaving the next page blank in my final version of this *TIRE ANNUAL*. But it doesn't have to be blank.

Ruth, That space is yours to fill any way you see fit. You can either say something or leave it blank. I'm taking my hands off the wheel. You can either grab it and steer or have a big old blank page that you can draw on, I guess.

It's up to you.

PS—Ruth, seriously. Do you have some weird shit in your will for me to do when you die?

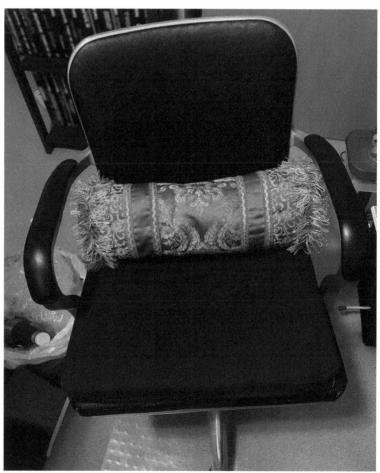

So, here's Arthur Peyton Corley's chair, modified for comfort. I never took him to be an ascetic guy, but you will get a very flat ass sitting in this thing for very long. Now it's the JIT's chair, or the Anti-JIT's chair. Regardless, it's at my house now.

Technically, this chair has been involved in creating more issues of TIRE than any human. Pretty soon it will get its own fan mail. It's the New Age version of "George Washington slept here."

Ruth, if you have nothing to say on the next page, your dad's empty chair gets the last word.—JIT

CPSIA information can be obtained
at www.ICGtesting.com
Printed in the USA
BVHW021343020821
613409BV00008B/110

9 780989 537131